D1461500

From Petticoat Tails
to Arbroath Smokies

Traditional Foods of Scotland

From Petticoat Tails to Arbroath Smokies

Traditional Foods of Scotland

Laura Mason and Catherine Brown
Foreword by Hugh Fearnley-Whittingstall

HarperPress
An imprint of HarperCollins*Publishers*

Harper*Press*
An imprint of HarperCollins*Publishers*
77–85 Fulham Palace Road
Hammersmith, London W6 8JB
www.harpercollins.co.uk

Published by Harper Press in 2007

First published in Great Britain in 1999
as part of *Traditional Foods of Britain*
by Prospect Books
Allaleigh House, Blackawton, Totnes, Devon TQ9 7DL
Copyright © 1999, 2004, edition and arrangement, Prospect Books
Copyright © 1999, text, GEIE/Euroterroirs, Paris

Subsequently published by Harper*Press* in 2006 as part of *The Taste of Britain*
Original design by 'OMEDESIGN
Copyright © 2007, edition and arrangement, Harper*Press*
Copyright © 2007, Foreword, Hugh Fearnley-Whittingstall
Copyright © 2007, Preface, Laura Mason and Catherine Brown
Copyright © contributions on p. 69-71/83-5/111/132-3 individual authors
(see Acknowledgements)

This edition produced for The Book People Ltd.,
Hall Wood Avenue, Haydock, St. Helens, WA11 9UL.

9 8 7 6 5 4 3 2 1

A catalogue record for this book
is available from the British Library

ISBN: 978-0-00-779-839-1

Design by Envy Design Ltd

Printed and bound in China

From Petticoat Tails to Arbroath Smokies is part of a series of books about regional British food which include:

From Bath Chaps to Bara Brith
The Taste of South West Britain

Bedfordshire Clangers and Lardy Cake
Traditional Foods from the South and South East

From Norfolk Knobs to Fidget Pie
Foods from the Heart of England and East Anglia

From Eccles Cake to Hawkshead Wig
A Celebration of Northern Food

These books originally formed part of the complete volume, *The Taste of Britain*, published by HarperPress in 2006.

Contents

Foreword by Hugh Fearnley-Whittingstall..*vii*
Preface ....*xiii*
Map of Britain..*xviii*

South Scotland...*1*
North Scotland..*59*
Scotland Countrywide *103*

Address Book...*159*
Bibliography *170*
Acknowledgements *172*

Foreword

Much is made these days of British food culture. Chefs and food writers, myself included, are keen to tell you that it's thriving, it should be celebrated, it's as good as anything our Continental cousins enjoy. Yet sometimes it seems as if our words come rolling back to us, as if bouncing off some distant landmass, unheard and unheeded along the way, so that we begin to have trouble persuading ourselves, let alone others, that there is something here worth fighting for.

The fact is that if you spend much time in supermarkets, or amongst the proliferation of branded fast foods on any high street, or if you eat in any but a handful of UK restaurants or pubs, then the concept of regional British food can seem a bit like Father Christmas, or Nirvana. A lovely romantic idea, but it doesn't really exist, does it?

Well, yes, it does. And if you're having trouble finding it, it may just be because you are looking in the wrong place. The problem, in part at least, is that the best, most uplifting stories about British food culture are being drowned out by the cacophony of mediocrity, and worse. The Turkey Twizzler is front page news – and rightly so, when it is making pre-basted, additive-laced butterballs of our children themselves. Shavings of Turkey 'ham' – 98 per cent fat free, of course – are filling the sandwiches of figure-conscious office workers the length and breadth of the nation. But the Norfolk Black, a real turkey slow-grown and bred for flavour, is out there, too – waiting to show you what he's worth. He's not making a song and dance – just gobbling quietly to himself. Track him down, and you're in for a revelation.

That's why this series of books are so timely, so necessary – and so brilliantly useful. They are a map, an investigative tool that will enable you to leave behind the homogenous and the bland, and set off on an exciting journey to find Britain's edible treasure – some of which may turn out to be hidden on your very doorstep.

I urge you not merely to browse them, but to use them. Because if you can get out there and discover for yourself some of our great British specialities – whether it's traditional sage Derby cheese, or the Yorkshire teacakes known as Fat Rascals, or a properly aged Suffolk cider vinegar – then you will discover, or at least remind yourself, that food can be so much more than fuel. That it can, several times a day, every day of our lives, relax us, stimulate us, and give us pleasure.

The foods described in this book can all work that small daily miracle of exciting our passions. Not all of them, for all of us. But each of them for some of us. They have been made and honed over generations – sometimes centuries – and they are still with us because enough of us – sometimes only just enough of us – love them. Of course, in many instances, we have yet to discover whether we love them or not. And that is why this book is so loaded with fantastic potential. Everybody has a new favourite food waiting for them in the pages ahead.

I've travelled fairly widely, if somewhat randomly, around Britain, and tracking down and tasting local foods has become an increasing priority for me. Very uplifting it is, too. Approach our regional food culture with a true sense of curiosity, and you can never become an old hand, or a jaded palate. I still feel a great sense of excitement and discovery when I finally get to eat a classic local dish on its own home turf. You can't easily deconstruct the magic formula of a well-made Lancashire Hot Pot, or a Dorset apple cake. It is in the nature of such dishes that their sum is greater than their parts. But you can, when you find a version that hits the spot, instantly appreciate how such dishes have survived the harsh natural selection of public taste, and come to delight, comfort and sustain families and groups of friends for so long.

Recently, for instance, I managed to track down my very first proper Yorkshire curd tart, its delectable filling made from colostrum – the very rich milk produced by a cow for her newborn calf. It was baked for me by a farmer's wife at home in her own kitchen, using the method passed down to her through her family, and it was wonderful – very rich, curdy and slightly crumbly – having a hint of cakiness without the flouriness (I told you deconstruction was a vain enterprise). Anyway, it was a world away from any 'regular' custard tart I'd tried before. What I learnt from that experience, and from many similar ones, is that regionality really does matter. If that tart had been made in Dorset or in the Highlands, it wouldn't have tasted the same. And if it had not been made at all, the world – and on that drizzly autumn day, me – would have been the poorer for it.

There are so many factors that affect the way a food turns out. Cheese is the best example. I love cheese – 'milk's leap toward immortality' as someone once said – and it never ceases to amaze me. It's made from milk, of course, plus something that will make the milk curdle (usually rennet, but sometimes quirkier coagulants, like nettle juice). Two basic ingredients. Yet cheese is one of the most diverse foods known to man. There are hundreds of varieties in the British Isles alone – and a bowlful of fresh, pillowy Scottish crowdie differs so greatly from a nutty Somerset cheddar that it's hard to believe they're basically the same stuff. The breed of cattle and their diet, the local water and pasture, the yeasts and bacteria that live locally in the air, the techniques used to curdle the milk, the way the cheese is pressed, turned, and aged – all these things affect the outcome.

That's why it seems absolutely right to me that only cheese made in a handful of Midlands dairies can be called Stilton, and that beer brewed with the gypsum-rich water in Burton-upon-Trent is labelled as such. What's more, if you understand why regional products are unique – that it's high temperatures and seaweed fertiliser that make Jersey Royals taste different to any other potatoes, for instance – then you know more about food in general. An understanding of regional diversity can only make us more intelligent and appreciative eaters.

This understanding is not always easy to come by. Most other European countries have long taken for granted that local foods should be protected, their unique identity preserved. Hence the French

AOC and the Italian DOC systems. But it's an idea not everyone in this country is comfortable with. I put this down to two things, and the first is the creeping curse of supermarket culture. The big multiple retailers try to tell us that we can eat whatever we want, whenever we want and indeed wherever we want. If you understand the seasonal nature of fresh produce, you know this is neither true nor desirable – and the same goes for regionality. You might not be able to buy genuine Arbroath smokies in every shop in the land, but that is precisely what makes them special when you do find them.

The second reason for resistance to regional labelling is illustrated by the pork pie issue. The pie makers of Melton Mowbray are currently battling to have their product awarded PGI (Protected Geographic Indication) status. That would mean only pies made in the area, to a traditional recipe, could carry the name. Other pork pie makers, from other areas, object to this. They want to call their products Melton Mowbray pies, too, arguing that their recipe is much the same. That's nonsense, of course: a recipe is only the beginning of a dish, a mere framework. The where, the how and the who of its making are just as important. But why would you even want to call your pie a Mowbray pie if it comes from London, or Swansea? Only, perhaps, if you know the real Mowbray pies taste better, and you can't be bothered to make your own recipe good enough to compete.

All of which goes to show why the issue of regionality is as relevant today as it ever has been. It's important not to see *From Petticoat Tails to Arbroath Smokies* as a history book, a compendium of nostalgic culinary whimsy. The food included here is alive and well, and there is nothing described in these pages that you can't eat today, as long as you go to the right place. That's perhaps the most important criterion for inclusion because our regional food traditions are just as much part of the future as the past. At least, they had better be, or we will be in serious trouble.

The implications for our health, and the health of our environment, are far-reaching. If we eat, say, fruit that's produced locally, not only do we reduce the food miles that are wrecking our climate, but that fruit will be fresher and richer in nutrients. If we can go to a butcher's shop to buy meat that's been raised nearby, we can ask the butcher how it was farmed, and how it was slaughtered. And perhaps we can take our children with us, so they learn something too. In the end, a local food culture, supplied in the main by contiguous communities, militates against secrecy, adulteration – cruelty even – and in favour of transparency, accountability and good practice. What could be more reassuring than knowing the names and addresses of the people who produce your food?

I don't think it's overstating the case, either, to say that a knowledge of regional cooking promotes resourcefulness and a renewed respect for food in all of us. Regional dishes are, by their very nature, simple things. This is folk cooking – a 'nose to tail' approach that uses whatever's available and makes it go as far as possible. For a while now – since conspicuous consumption has become practically an end in itself – our predecessors' abhorrence of throwing away anything may have seemed at best, quaint, at worst, laughable. But as we begin to come to terms with the consequences of our 'have it all now' culture, it is becoming clear that ethical production, good husbandry, environmental responsibility and kitchen thrift all go hand in hand. The frugal culture that gave birth to chitterlings and lardy cake, Bath chaps and bread pudding is something we should be proud to belong to. To re-embrace it can only do us good.

Aside from their currency, the foods in this book have had to prove themselves in other ways. They must be unique to a specific region and they must have longevity, having been made or produced for at least 75 years. Finally, they must be, to use a rather ugly word, 'artisanal'. That means that special knowledge and skills are required to make them properly. Which brings me to one crucial element of good food that should never be forgotten: the people who make it. Almost without exception, the brewers, bakers, cooks, farmers and fishermen who produce traditional foods are what you might call 'characters'. This doesn't mean they are yokels caught in a yesteryear time warp. They are people of passion and commitment, intelligence and good humour, and often extraordinary specialist knowledge. And they know more than most of us about the meaning of life.

Not a single one of them goes to work in the morning in order to make lots of money – you certainly don't choose to devote your life to bannock-making in the hope it will furnish you with a swimming pool and a Ferrari. They do it because they believe in it and, ultimately, feel it is worthwhile. In their own quiet and industrious way, they understand just how much is at stake. The future of civilized, communal, respectful life on our islands? It is not preposterous to suggest it. Use your regular custom and generously expressed enthusiasm to support this modest army of dedicated souls, working away in their kitchens, gardens, orchards breweries and smokehouses all over Britain, and you do a great deal more than simply save a cheese, or a beer, for posterity. You help save the next generation from the tyranny of industrial mediocrity.

Amid this talk of pride and principles, it's crucial not to lose sight of the fact that this is food to be enjoyed, celebrated – and shared with friends. Dishes don't survive down the centuries unless they taste good. You may not need much persuasion to try some of the buttery cakes or fabulously fresh fruit and veg described in these pages. But you will perhaps need a sense of adventure to rediscover the charms of some of the entries. Be ready to cast your squeamishness aside and sample some tripe, some tongue, some trotters as well. If the experience of visitors to our River Cottage events here in Dorset is anything to go by, I'm betting you'll be pleasantly surprised. You'll be taking a pig's head home from the butcher's and making your own brawn before you can say, 'Er, not for me, thanks.'

One element of this series of books to be richly savoured is the language. They are written, by Laura Mason and Catherine Brown, without hyperbole, but with a precision and clarity that far better express their authors' underlying passion and purpose. Another thing that makes them a joy to read is their embrace of the regional food vernacular: Dorset knobs, Puggie Buns, Singin' Hinnies, Black Bullets and Mendip Wallfish are all to be revelled in for their names alone. Indeed, some might be tempted to enjoy them chiefly as a glorious catalogue of eccentricity, a celebration of the cowsheel and the careless gooseberry, of the head cheese and the damson cheese (neither of which are actually cheese) that make this country's food so charming and idiosyncratic.

But to do so would be to miss out. Now that this book exists, now that it is in your hands, use it to bring about change. It should not be taken as a slice of the past, in aspic, but as a well-stocked store cupboard, with the potential to enrich our future food culture. See it not as a preservation order for British regional foods, but a call to action. Use this book as a guide, not merely to seek out delicious things that you've never tried before, but also to recreate some of them in your own kitchen. Do that and you'll be actively participating in a great food culture that has always been with us, that is often hidden beneath the mass-produced, homogenous, seasonless food we are so frequently offered, but which may yet have a vibrant future.

This book - along with the others in the series - is a thorough and splendid answer to the question 'What is British food?' Use it well, and it may help to ensure that is still a meaningful question a hundred years from now.

Hugh Fearnley-Whittingstall

Preface

In 1994 we embarked on a mission to describe as many British foods with regional affiliations as we could find. We were part of a Europe-wide project working within a framework – handed down from Brussels – which demanded a link to the *terroir* (soil). In fact the project, named Euroterroir, was more suited to rural southern Europe than industrialized, urbanized Britain. How do you link Yorkshire Relish to the soil? But ultimately we succeeded in writing up some four hundred British entries. And along the way we asked some broader questions – what are our traditional foods? What is the character of British taste?

We've discovered that many rural treasures had survived against the odds. That sometimes foods with traditional or regional affiliations languished unloved. That sometimes British foods, though not always linking directly to the *terroir*, did have other powerful historical influences which made them special, and distinct, from the rest of Europe. No other country in Europe has a history of spicing to match the British.

Yet our homogenized food supply was clearly inflicting a far-reaching loss of local distinctiveness and quality. The idea, inherent in the project, that foods should be the property of a place and its community (*terroir*, in the context of food in France, carries implications of regionality, cultural groupings and the influence of trade and climate), rather than the trademarked possession of an individual or company, was especially alien.

Our initial research complete, we felt confident that either the Ministry of Agriculture or Food from Britain would take up the cause and publish a book based on the work which had taken us two years to complete. Instead, it was a small publisher in Devon (Tom Jaine of

Prospect Books) who kept the flag flying and *Traditional Foods of Britain* was published in 1999. Eight years on, we welcome this series published by HarperCollins.

We also welcome signs of change. Now, there is more awareness of commercial dilution, and dishonest imitation and therefore the need to protect food names, though the application process for producers is slow and difficult. There are certainly more small producers working locally, but they have to cope with numerous barriers. However much they protest otherwise, powerful supermarket central distribution systems and cut-throat pricing polices are not designed to foster local produce. And consumers do not always pause to consider the more subtle and elusive nuances of foods from closer to home.

Of course the ties of regionality do not suit foodstuffs, and in any case should be just one of many avenues open to British farmers and food producers. But it would be good to see more raw local ingredients transformed into distinctive foods since records show their rich variety in the past. Shops and markets bursting with colourful and varied local produce are one of the great pleasures of shopping for food on the continent. They exist because national policies and local custom support them. They should not be impossible in Britain. These books are not an end, but a beginning.

Laura Mason and Catherine Brown 2007

THE BRITISH
ISLES

0 10 20 30 40 50 60
British Miles

ATLANTIC OCEAN

2

INVERNESS   ABERDEEN

1

DUNDEE

EDINBURGH

GLASGOW

NEWCASTLE

NORTH SEA

IRISH SEA

LEEDS

MANCHESTER

LIVERPOOL

SHEFFIELD

ST. GEORGE'S CHANNEL

BIRMINGHAM

NORWICH

SWANSEA

CARDIFF   BRISTOL

LONDON

SOUTHAMPTON

PLYMOUTH

THE ENGLISH CHANNEL

Regions

1. *South Scotland*

2. *North Scotland*

South Scotland: East, South, Central & Borders

Kale

KALE HAS NO HEART BUT GROWS ON A LONG STEM WITH CURLED FINELY DENTED LEAVES. COLOUR: DARK GREEN. FLAVOUR: CHANGES FROM MILD TO MORE INTENSELY SPICY AFTER IT HAS BEEN FROSTED.

HISTORY:

Kale was originally a staple, surviving well in a harsh winter, consumed throughout northern Europe. The word cole, i.e. kale, used generically for members of the brassica family, stems first from the Latin, *caulis*. Similar derivations are widespread in European languages, from the Welsh *cawl*, to the German *Kohl*. Borecole is curly kale, an improved variety taken from the Dutch, where it was called *boerenkool*, 'peasant's cabbage'. In the same way, hearted cabbage was sometimes called cabbage-cole (from the French *caboche*, head).

The kail-yard (kitchen garden) was to the Scots (particularly in the Lowlands) what the potato-plot was to the Irish peasant. Kail was so inextricably linked with eating, that the midday meal became known as 'kail'. The bells of St Giles Cathedral in Edinburgh which chimed at dinner-time (in the eighteenth century at 2 o'clock) were known as the 'Kail-bells'. In Meg Dods (1826), Scotland is referred to as 'The Land o' Kail'. So attached is the word to a particular vision of the country that 'kail-yaird' has been applied to a school of fiction which depicts Scottish village life. Two practitioners were Sir James Barrie and S.R. Crockett.

While the Scots used the spelling kail, the northern English called it cale. Today, it is known in Scotland and the rest of Britain as kale and the Scots continue to use it in broths, or as a vegetable, while in England it has largely remained winter feed for cattle.

TECHNIQUE:

The advantage of kale for Scottish growers is that it is hardy. Also, it has the rare quality in a vegetable of benefiting from periods of frost. In a normal Scottish winter, several frosts, the duration and number depending on altitude, aspect and the general weather, can be expected, so any vegetable resistant to these is useful.

Traditional varieties such as Green Curled and Thousand Headed Kale are little grown, although efforts to preserve their genetic material is carried on by a dedicated band. F1 hybrids, which crop uniformly and reliably, are now favoured. Commercially, kale is grown from seed in mid-May to early July for winter use. It is less hardy in rich soils. Older methods of growing survived in the Orkneys into the 1970s, the seed being sown in plantie crubs – specially constructed enclosures of turf or stone in the common grazings. In April, the growing plants were transferred to kaleyards near the houses to grow on to maturity (Fenton, 1973).

REGION OF PRODUCTION:

GENERAL SCOTLAND, SOUTH EAST SCOTLAND, FIFE AND LOTHIAN.

Leek (Scotland)

DESCRIPTION:

COLOUR: WHITE STEM, DARK GREEN LEAVES. FLAVOUR: SWEET, LESS PUNGENT THAN ONIONS. A SCOTTISH LEEK WILL HAVE ALMOST AS MUCH GREEN AS WHITE, WHILE 'LONG BLANCHED' LEEKS WITH ONLY A VERY SHORT GREEN FLAG ARE MORE TYPICALLY ENGLISH.

HISTORY:

Leeks are the dominant vegetable in cock-a-leekie, a Scottish national dish. It is broth made with fowl and leeks, first developed in the

Lowlands. The earliest known reference is in the Ochtertyre House book (*c.* 1737). Success depends to a large extent on the quality of leeks. The dish flourished, certainly in Edinburgh taverns, as a direct result of the market gardens on the fertile soils along the Lothian coast which supplied the city with vegetables and fruits and were renowned for the fine quality of their leeks. A variety of the Common Long Winter Leek, raised near Edinburgh and possessing a longer, thicker stem and broad leaves, is described as a 'Poireau de Musselbourgh' [Musselburgh, Lothian] by William Robinson in *The Vegetable Garden* (1885): 'The fine qualities of this vegetable are much better known to the Welsh, Scotch and French than to the English or Irish.'

Scots leeks are distinguished from others by their long leaf (green flag) and short blanch (white). The large amount of green is necessary to give broths a good colour. Because it is sweeter and more delicate than the onion, it is often described as the 'king of the soup onions'.

TECHNIQUE:
Leeks are grown from seed in rich, well-drained soils. Fife and Lothian, lowland areas with fertile, light soils, continue to be important. Small to medium-sized leeks have the sweetest flavour. The Musselburgh is grown by some amateurs though no longer commercially.

REGION OF PRODUCTION:
CENTRAL AND EAST SCOTLAND.

Raspberry (Scottish)

DESCRIPTION:
VISUAL AND TASTE DIFFERENCES BETWEEN THE 3 MAIN VARIETIES OF SCOTTISH RASP-BERRY ARE MINIMAL: CLOVA IS A MEDIUM-SIZED, LIGHT- TO MEDIUM-COLOURED FRUIT WITH A SWEETISH-SHARP FLAVOUR; PROSEN IS A LARGER FRUIT, MEDIUM RED-COLOURED AND IS GENERALLY REGARDED TO HAVE A SOURER FLAVOUR BUT IS FIRMER AND MORE EASILY TRANSPORTABLE; MOY IS A LARGE BERRY, MEDIUM RED

COLOUR, GENERALLY REGARDED AS THE BEST FLAVOURED, BUT THE MOST DIFFICULT TO GROW.

HISTORY:

The English name comes from the Old English *raspis*, a word of obscure origin, probably connected with the slightly hairy, rasping surface of the fruit. Grown in Europe for centuries, it was not until the seventeenth that British horticulturists began to take the fruit seriously and cookery books started including recipes for raspberry wine and vinegar. Though also grown commercially in England, it was a group of Scottish market gardeners in Angus at the beginning of the twentieth century who decided, because of the damp climate, to move out of strawberry production. They joined together as a co-operative growing raspberries commercially and eventually made the Scottish crop the dominant British supply.

In 1946 the Scottish Raspberry Investigation was set up at University College, Dundee, transferring to Mylnefield Farm at Invergowrie in 1951 when the Scottish Crop Research Institute was set up as a horticultural research station in the heart of raspberry-growing country. Over the years it has supported the industry and been largely instrumental in its success by developing varieties with a view to increasing yields, producing disease-resistant plants, improving flavour and retaining quality. All of this has made this the major raspberry growing area in Britain and the SCRI the lead centre for British research on soft fruits.

The very successful raspberry breeding programme at SCRI is best known for the 'Glen' series of cultivars which are now grown throughout the world. The first of the series was Glen Clova (1970) and was a mainstay of the raspberry industry. Glen Moy (1981) was the first spine-free raspberry. Glen Prosen was also released in 1981, and Glen Ample in 1996. Other minor varieties are Glen Garry (1990); Glen Lyon (1991); and Glencoe (1989), a purple raspberry. Autumn-fruiting Autumn Bliss is also grown, serving a niche consumer market. SCRI cultivars occupy 96 per cent of the raspberry market in Scotland.

The distribution of the crop is between the various sectors of the market: fresh; punnet-frozen; quick-frozen in bulk; canned; puréed. Recently, the allocation to canned and puréed production has declined while there has been an increase in fresh and frozen.

TECHNIQUE:

Scottish growers turned to their advantage a cooler climate and shorter growing season, combined with the fertile soils of the East coast, in an area favoured for farming ever since it was cultivated by monks in the Middle Ages. Raspberries are grown outdoors on rows of posts at 10-metre spacing; these are joined by double wires running parallel and clipped together with small metal clips; individual fruiting canes are tied with twine to a single wire further up the posts, about 1.4 metres above the ground. Canes are propagated by suckers from the parent plant. The fruit matures slowly, benefiting from the dryish summers and long periods of midsummer daylight rather than any great heat. Mid-season varieties crop on two-year-old canes. They may be harvested mechanically or by hand.

REGION OF PRODUCTION:

EAST SCOTLAND, TAYSIDE; NORTH EAST SCOTLAND, MORAYSHIRE; SOUTH SCOTLAND, BORDERS.

Swede-Turnip

DESCRIPTION:

A ROOT VEGETABLE WITH A WOODY OUTER SKIN, USUALLY SOLD FOR DOMESTIC CONSUMPTION AT 1–2KG WEIGHT. FOR CATTLE AND SHEEP FEEDING IN WINTER, THEY ARE GROWN MUCH LARGER, WHEN THEY BECOME TOUGH AND COARSE-FLAVOURED. COLOUR: DARK BROWN TO PURPLE ON OUTER SKIN, PALE YELLOW TO ORANGE INSIDE. FLAVOUR: SWEETISH, MILD SPICINESS WHEN YOUNG AND SMALL, THE FLAVOUR DETERIORATES IN LARGE SPECIMENS.

HISTORY:

While the Romans were responsible for introducing the English

white turnip, *Brassica rapa*, the yellow turnip, *Brassica campestris*, came to Scotland in the late 1700s. English farming experiments had led to the development of root crops for feeding to cattle during the winter, among them the yellow turnip or swede from Bohemia (rather than Sweden [Stobart, 1980]). The Scots took to the yellow turnip as a vegetable for human consumption more enthusiastically than the English. In Scotland it is known as neeps (a shortening of turnip); rutabaga is its American name, deriving from the Swedish dialect name *rotbagga*; and in England it is known as Swedish turnip or swede. The turnip is generally used in England for the white turnip (French *navet*). 'Our club,' said Meg Dods (1826), 'put powdered gineger [sic] to their mashed turnips, which were studiously chosen of the yellow, sweet, juicy sort, for which Scotland is celebrated.' This appreciation was otherwise only shared by some in northern England.

Mashed turnips, or bashed neeps, became the accepted accompaniment to haggis at Burns' suppers, along with mashed potatoes (champit tatties). In the Islands and parts of the Highlands where both potatoes and turnips are grown they were often mixed together as the main dish of the day in an eating tradition largely devoid of meat. In Orkney mixed potato and turnip was called clapshot, a word whose origin is unknown. It is now common through-out the country, frequently eaten with haggis.

TECHNIQUE:

The plants withstand cold winters and are hardier than English white turnips, making them a useful vegetable in the northern chill before the development of modern transport and distribution systems for fresh vegetables. They grow well in light, rich soils; they are grown from seed, normally sown in May for production mid-August to April. A relatively early sowing date is necessary in the north as it gives a longer growing season. Magres is the dominant variety grown in Scotland, other established varieties are Acme, Doon Major and Ruta Otofte. Newer varieties include Ruby and Joan. For processing, some

Laurentian (pale-fleshed) and Merrick (white-fleshed) are grown. The main growing districts are on the eastern side of the country, from East Aberdeenshire to the Lothians.

REGION OF PRODUCTION:
SCOTLAND.

Tomato (Clyde Valley)

DESCRIPTION:

A TOMATO WITH RED SKIN AND FLESH AND A WELL-BALANCED TART SWEETNESS WITH A PLEASING BITE.

HISTORY:

A sheltered valley with fertile soils and a mild West-coast climate, with easy access to the largest and densest area of population in Scotland, provided the right conditions for the development of fruit and vegetable growing in the Clyde Valley. Once markets were assured, with the growth of population in the late nineteenth century, horticultural crops flourished, among them tomatoes. Though not traditionally a crop grown in northern climates, those from the Clyde were widely acclaimed for their intense, pleasing flavour and commanded a premium price as 'Scotch Tomatoes'.

Since tomato growing had depended largely on the use of cheap fuel to heat the glasshouses, the increase in the price of oil at the beginning of the 1970s meant that the growers could no longer produce economically. For the next couple of decades tomato growing practically died out. Its revival in the 1990s was largely due to the development of the marketing consortium 'Scotland's Tomatoes', a group of 5 of the largest growers who invested in new and more efficient nurseries, combined with a promotional effort to re-establish Clyde Valley tomatoes as a high-quality product.

Part of the success of this venture is due to enhanced flavour because the fruit can be left on the vine until much later than most other tomatoes which must be picked under-ripe to allow the time necessary for transportation. The Clyde Valley tomato is fresher, better-tasting, and more naturally ripened.

The variety which was largely responsible for the early 'Scotch Tomatoes', known as Ailsa Craig, is no longer grown since it was not disease resistant. Growers have developed others to suit the climate and growing season. The most widely cultivated is Spectra.

TECHNIQUE:
Mostly grown in a hydroponic system in bags of perlite or in long narrow channels containing a stream of nutrients, the plants rely solely on a liquid solution for nourishment. Air temperature and humidity are carefully controlled. Bumble bees are used to pollinate.

REGION OF PRODUCTION:
CENTRAL SCOTLAND.

Vegetarian Haggis

DESCRIPTION:
FORM: AN OVAL BALL SHAPE. WEIGHT: 75G–2KG. COLOUR: GREYISH CREAM. FLAVOUR: NUTTY-MEALY, SAVOURY, NOT HIGHLY SPICED.

HISTORY:
Haggis is now considered an exclusively Scottish dish based on sheep offal though recipes were once plentiful in English cookery texts (see Haggis p.118). These show that the ingredients have varied over the years. In the seventeenth century a meatless 'Haggas Pudding in a Sheep's Paunch' requires parsley, savoury, thyme, onions, beef suet, oatmeal, cloves, mace, pepper and salt while a 'sweet' meatless haggis recipe has been handed down through the writer's family for 4 generations. Something akin to the Hebridean 'Marag', it is made with flour, oatmeal, beef suet, dried fruit, and a little sugar, and steamed in a cloth (cloot) like a clootie dumpling (p.111, 131). Though the marag ingredients are the same, the sweet haggis is less solid, more crumbly in texture and arguably more palatable. Another mention of a similar meatless Scottish haggis is in Hartley (1954) under the description of

'Gold Belly' which she describes as a version of an 'English oatmeal pudding, Scotch mountain recipe'.

In 1984 Edinburgh butcher John MacSween was challenged by a vegetarian poet, Tessa Ransford, to make a haggis for the Burns' Supper held to open the Scottish Poetry Library. After a number of experiments, he developed a recipe based on lentils, beans, oatmeal and vegetables. The enthusiastic response from guests and press encouraged him to make the haggis commercially, taking the old idea of the meatless haggis but using a plastic casing rather than a sheep's stomach bag. Output increased steadily every year. The haggis needs reheating only and is eaten, as customary, with tatties and neeps or with clapshot. 'Haggis meat,' said Meg Dods (1826), 'for those who do not admire the natural shape, may be poured out of the bag, and served in a deep dish.' It may also be sliced and fried or grilled and eaten with bacon and eggs for breakfast.

TECHNIQUE:
Lentils, black beans, onions and oatmeal are soaked in water overnight. Mushrooms, turnips and carrots are prepared and put through a fine mincer with the black beans. The mixture then goes through a coarser mincer with the lentils; oatmeal and onions, seasoning and melted margarine are added and mixed. The mixture is then fed into the skins which are sealed and boiled in water.

REGION OF PRODUCTION:
SCOTLAND, EDINBURGH.

Ayrshire Milk

HISTORY:
The Ayrshire breed of milk cow is thought to have developed during the seventeenth century. There are few early records of any sort of milk production. Cattle were kept as draught animals, for tallow and for fresh and salt beef. The dairy cow was first noted in the Cunningham district of north Ayrshire in a report of 1794 for the

Board of Agriculture: 'In Cunningham, a breed of cattle has for more than a century been established, remarkable for the quantity and quality of their milk in proportion to their size. They have long been denominated the Dunlop breed, from family and place of that name, where great attention was paid to milk yields and quality.'

Though the qualities of the native stock were the foundation of the breed, it is likely that there was some crossing with blood from elsewhere. The first Ayrshire Herd Book was set up in 1877. Though some early portraits of Ayrshires depict oxen and other fatstock, it has been a dairy breed for most of its history and certainly established itself as such throughout the nineteenth century when most cattle husbandry in Britain was oriented towards beef.

A vital factor in its development was the butter and cheese industry of South-West Scotland. When the cheese industry slowed down in the 1880s, the response of the dairy farmers within easy distance of the big cities of central Scotland was to switch to liquid milk supply. Managed and distributed by the Milk Marketing Board from 1933, the distinctive character of milk from Ayrshire herds was lost and has only been revived with the disbandment of controls in 1994, giving renewed opportunity for milk from specific herds to be marketed separately.

Ayrshire milk has a minimum butterfat content of 4 per cent. It is bought by those with a preference for a deeper-flavoured milk; it has a higher protein and lactose content which gives it a richer, sweeter taste. The fat globules are also smaller and more uniform which is known to make the milk more digestible that some other milks.

REGION OF PRODUCTION:
SCOTLAND, AYRSHIRE (STRATHCLYDE).

Dunlop Cheese

DESCRIPTION:

PASTEURIZED, HARD, COW'S MILK CHEESE, DISTINGUISHED FROM
SCOTTISH CHEDDAR AS 'MEATIER', WITH A MORE MELLOW, NUTTY
FLAVOUR AND SOFTER, CREAMIER TEXTURE. COLOUR: PALE YELLOW.
FORM: ROUNDS FROM 2KG.

HISTORY:

The lowlands of Ayrshire form a crescent along 70 miles of the Firth of Clyde. The warm, wet winds, and the clay and heavy loam soil have combined to grow the most succulent pasture, making this the largest dairying area in the country and the home of Ayrshire cattle, first known as Dunlops or Cunninghams.

Until the late seventeenth century, cheese had been essentially a short-keeping by-product of butter-making, made from the skimmed milk of both cow and sheep. Around 1690, however, a farmer's daughter and Covenanter from Ayrshire, Barbara Gilmour, is said to have returned home after a period of exile in Ulster fleeing religious persecution. She brought with her a recipe for making cheese which revolutionized the product. Instead of using skimmed milk, she used full-cream cow's milk, pressing the cheese until it was quite hard and improving both the keeping quality and the flavour. While the old cheese was described as 'common cheese', the new cheese became known as 'sweet-milk cheese' or 'new milk cheese'. By the 1790s, when parish accounts were compiled for the Statistical Account of Scotland, it had become a Dunlop cheese, identified as being manufactured in 5 Ayrshire and 2 Lanarkshire parishes.

The rise of Dunlop to more than local significance relates to the growth of the cities of central Scotland, particularly Glasgow and Paisley. The cheese was further improved in 1885 when the Ayrshire Agricultural Association brought a Somerset farmer and his wife to the country to teach the Cheddar method. Original Dunlop was still being made by at least 300 farms in the South-West of Scotland in 1930: 'Each farm had a fully matured cheese open for cooking, and a softer one for eating. At breakfast, porridge was followed on alternate days by bacon and eggs or toasted cheese on a scone made of home-ground flour eaten in front of the fire' (Rance, 1982).

The subsequent decline – though not extinction – of Dunlop was a result of developments during and after World War II: milk was bought in bulk from farms by Milk Marketing Boards (MMB) and trucked to large creameries to make factory Cheddar. Its position was further undermined when the MMB took Cheddar rather than Dunlop as the name for their creamery cheeses, believing that Dunlop presented the wrong image, since it happened to have the same name as a leading rubber tyre company of the day, now defunct. Only in some creameries, notably on some of the islands, particularly on Arran, did they retain the Dunlop name and tradition. Elsewhere, Scottish cheese took the Cheddar tag though there have been moves recently to restore Dunlop to its traditional role as a Scottish cheese of distinguished ancestry.

TECHNIQUE:

Made from pasteurized cow's milk. Commercially, it follows the basic Cheddar method but is pressed for a shorter time and matured 4–12 months (average 6 months). An historical recipe is given by McNeill (1929): 'As soon as the milk is taken from the cows it is poured into a large pail, or pails, and before it is quite cold the substance called the steep, i.e. rennet, is mixed with it. When it is sufficiently coagulated it is cut transversely with a broad knife made for the purpose, or a broad three-toed instrument, in order to let the curd subside and to procure the separation of the whey from it. When this separation is observed to have taken place, the curd is lifted with a ladle, or something similar, into the chessel where it remains a few hours, till it has acquired something of a hardness or consistency. It is then taken out of the cheese press and cut into small pieces with the instrument above mentioned, of the size of one or 2 cubic inches, after which it receives the due proportion of salt, and is again replaced in the chessel and put into the press, where it remains a few hours again. Then it is taken out a second time, cut as before and mixed thoroughly, so that every part may receive the benefit of the salt; and for the last time it is put into the cheese press where it remains till replaced by its successor. After this is done it must be laid in a clean and cool place till sufficiently dried and fit to be carried to market; great care is to be used in frequent turning and rubbing, both to keep the cheese dry and clean and to preserve it from swelling and bursting with the heat, vulgarly "fire-fanging". When these cheeses are properly made and dried as they ought to be, they have a rich and delicious flavour.'

REGION OF PRODUCTION:
SCOTLAND, AYRSHIRE, SOUTH WEST AND SOME ISLANDS.

Dunsyre Blue Cheese

DESCRIPTION:
A ROUND, UNPASTEURIZED, BLUE-VEINED COW'S MILK CHEESE. WEIGHT: 3KG. COLOUR: CREAM OR WHITE WITH BLUE VEINS. FLAVOUR: CREAMY, SHARP WITH LONG AFTERTASTE.

HISTORY:
A tradition of artisan farmhouse cheeses, dating back at least to the 1600s, flourished in the dairying areas of the south of Scotland until World War II. Other entries (see Dunlop, above) touch on the reasons for its decline.

Dunsyre Blue is an artisan-made cheese which has gained a considerable reputation. It is made by Humphrey Errington in Lanarkshire. In the 1990s he set up a group of artisan cheese-makers as a marketing co-op called the Hand-made Cheeses of Scotland Group, taking cheeses to trade fairs and other promotional occasions.

TECHNIQUE:
Made from unpasteurized milk from a herd of Ayrshire cows. The milk is started with an inoculation of bacteria and penicillin followed by vegetarian rennet which sets the curd. The curd is cut and drained. 4–4.5kg of curd is packed into moulds and left to settle without pressure for 4 days. The cheeses are dipped in brine, rubbed with salt

and, after 6 days, pierced to develop the mould. Maturing is over about 3 months during which time they are turned every day and, when necessary, will be wrapped in foil to prevent surface mould developing.

REGION OF PRODUCTION:
SCOTLAND, LANARKSHIRE.

Kelsae Cheese

DESCRIPTION:
HARD, PRESSED, UNPASTEURIZED COW'S MILK CHEESE. THERE ARE 2 TYPES, KELSAE AND STITCHILL; THEY COME IN SEVERAL SIZES, 500G–6.5KG. FLAVOUR: BOTH HAVE A RICHNESS DERIVED FROM THE JERSEY MILK; KELSAE HAS A SHARP NOTE; STITCHILL IS MILD AND CREAMY.

HISTORY:
See the entry for Bonchester, above, for the fall and rise of farmhouse cheese-making in Scotland. Brenda Leddy is a Yorkshire dairy-woman who moved to Kelso (Borders). In approximately 1988, she began making the cheeses Stitchill and Kelsae (the old name for Kelso) from a herd of 25–32 Jersey cows. Both recipes were given to her by artisan cheesemakers in the Highlands (their origin and history is unknown) but she has altered and developed them to suit the Jersey milk, while retaining the characteristics of the originals. A cream cheese, known as Stitchill Soft, is made by the same farm.

TECHNIQUE:
Kelsae and Stitchill are made from unpasteurized milk from a herd of Jersey cows. The method for both is similar but varies in detail. Curdling: with bacterial starter (Stitchill), with yoghurt (Kelsae), followed by rennet which sets the curd in about an hour. Cutting: the curd is cut and heated in a hot-water bath to the correct acidity. (Kelsae is only just warmed, Stitchill is heated to hand-hot.) It is cooled and drained, left overnight, milled, salted and mixed. The curd is poured into cheesecloth-lined moulds and pressed for 3–4 days. It is

matured for 5–7 months. The season runs from spring to autumn.

REGION OF PRODUCTION:
SCOTLAND, BORDERS.

Lanark Blue Cheese

DESCRIPTION:

A ROUND, UNPASTEURIZED, BLUE-VEINED EWE'S MILK CHEESE. WEIGHT: 3KG. COLOUR: CREAM TO WHITE, MOTTLED WITH BLUE VEINS. FLAVOUR: SHARP YET CREAMY, WITH A LONG AFTERTASTE.

HISTORY:

The original stronghold of ewe's milk cheese appears to have been the Border counties. Here it survived at least into the early nineteenth century: 'the much deforested Forest of Ettrick in Selkirkshire was one of the areas in which ewe's milk cheese was still of importance. The parish of Ettrick, to which no reliably passable roads then led, exported mutton and cheese to the market fifteen miles off from its flocks of 30,000 sheep, whose fleece was too coarse for wool buyers' (Rance, 1982). Better-keeping and better-tasting cheese from cow's milk was the main reason for its decline. (See Dunlop, p.11.)

Lanark Blue and its maker, Humphrey Errington, have been of the first importance in guiding the course of events. Lanark Blue has become recognized as a gourmet cheese, classed for quality and type beside Roquefort.

TECHNIQUE:

Milk from a Friesland-cross dairy flock is used. It is started with an inoculation of bacteria and penicillin followed by vegetarian rennet which sets the curd. This is cut and drained; 4–4.5kg is packed into moulds and left to settle without pressure for 4 days. The cheese is dipped in brine, rubbed with salt and, after 6 days, pierced to develop the mould. Maturing takes place over about 3 months. The cheeses are turned every day and, when necessary, will be wrapped in foil to prevent surface mould developing.

REGION OF PRODUCTION:
SCOTLAND, LANARKSHIRE.

Italian (Tally's) Ice-Cream

DESCRIPTION:
CLASSIC SCOTTISH 'ITALIAN' VANILLA ICE-CREAM IS USUALLY MADE ENTIRELY OF MILK AND IS THEREFORE LESS CREAMY THAN THOSE ICES WITH A RICHER CREAM CONTENT. IT IS ALSO SLIGHTLY COLDER AND MORE ICY, TAKING LONGER TO FREEZE. THIS GIVES IT AN INCREASED DENSITY, WHICH HAS THE EFFECT OF INTENSIFYING THE FLAVOUR TO SOMETHING WHICH IS CLEAR, CLEAN, LIGHT AND WHOLLY MILKY.

HISTORY:
This is the product of the 'Tallys', Italian cafés which are a feature of Scottish high streets. The first Italians came to Britain in the 1850s but, by the end of the century, as economic conditions worsened in Italy, the trickle of immigrants became a flood. Recruited by agents of masters in London, they were hired as cheap labour. In winter they worked as hurdy-gurdy men, but in summer they cranked and froze the ice-cream mix they had made the previous night.

According to Bruno Sereni in *They Took the Low Road* (1973), the first Italians to arrive in Glasgow were from the Ciociana district, and they were responsible for laying the foundations of what was to become a flourishing ice-cream (and fish-and-chip) industry in Scotland. 'With great courage and initiative, in the space of about seventy years (1850–1920), they had graduated from itinerant begging … to itinerant ice-cream salesmen … to owners of shops in slum quarters … to proprietors of luxurious ice-cream parlours in Sauchiehall Street with mirrors on the walls and wooden partitions between the leather-covered seats.'

As the Italian ice-cream trade developed, a hierarchy was established with the most prosperous playing a major role in the training and careers of many of the young immigrants. They started at the bottom of the ladder and worked up to the ownership of a shop. Itinerant ice-cream selling continued (as it still does) but many more Italian cafés were opened, often as part of a chain. Then the individual shops were sold off to employees when they showed that they could make a profit.

This large community of quality Italian ice-cream makers spread themselves about Scotland to such an extent that every town had at least one, if not two, Italian cafés (nicknamed Tallys). Robert McKee (1991) gave figures which reflect their growing importance: in 1903 there were 89 in Glasgow, a year later 184, and by 1905, 336. Italian ice-cream had become one of the great pleasures of the working classes, and was soon to become socially acceptable to the prissy middle classes as well. Young men like Denis in A.J. Cronin's novel about Glasgow, *Hatter's Castle*, started taking their girlfriends to the forbidden territory of the Tally. Cronin's Mary had expected to find a 'sordid den', but instead there were clean marble-topped tables, shining mirrors, plush stalls and, best of all, seductive ice-cream.

A range of ices became popular, with some borrowing from the American sundae tradition, but most distinctive and persistent was the habit of pouring a raspberry sauce over the ice-cream. One legend has it that it was invented in Glasgow when a supporter of Clyde football club, whose colours are red and white, persuaded his Tally to make a red and white ice-cream. The ice-cream was named 'Macallum' after the supporter. Special 'Macallum Saucers' are remembered, though the raspberry sauce (commonly known as Tally's Blood) is now mostly poured over cones.

The extent to which Scottish tastes have been influenced by this quality ice-cream can be seen in its continued popularity. Before the discovery of soft-scoop ice-cream – made with the maximum amount of air which can be beaten in to increase the volume because it is sold by volume not weight – a post-war generation of Scottish children had tasted the real thing. They had queued at their local Tallys, if not with the family milk-jug for a fill-up of ice-cream in the days when no one had a refrigerator, then certainly for a penny-cone dripping with bright red Tally's blood. The soft-scoop 'whippy' ices were no match for the Tally's ice-cream.

The ingredients are first pasteurized, i.e. heated at varying temperatures from 60°C upwards. They are then homogenized under pressure, the degree of pressure depending on the percentage of solids in the mix. The mixture is cooled quickly through chilled coils, it is then put into an 'ageing' vat where, again depending on the percentage of solids, the mixture is left to mature. It is then put into the freezer, which may be a batch-type taking about 25 litres at a time, or a continuous freezer. In the batch-type, 40 per cent (and upwards) of air is beaten into the ice-cream; in the continuous freezer it is pumped in. If the amount of air added exceeds 100 per cent, the subsequent amount is known as 'overrun'. Italian ice-cream manufacturers are reluctant to declare the exact percentage of air added, but maintain it is much less than 100 per cent but not quite as low as 40 per cent.

REGION OF PRODUCTION:
CENTRAL SCOTLAND.

Arbroath Smokie

DESCRIPTION:

A HOT-SMOKED, HEADED, GUTTED, UNFILLETED HADDOCK. WEIGHT: 250G–300G. COLOUR: COPPER-BROWN ON OUTSIDE, FLESH INSIDE CREAMY WHITE. FLAVOUR: MELLOW OVERTONES OF SALT AND SMOKE.

HISTORY:

First developed in Auchmithie, a fishing village a little north of Arbroath, this was originally known as an Auchmithie lucken or close fish or pinwiddie. Auchmithie was largely populated by families of Norse origin. Their names still bear the evidence. The Norse-descended Spink family owns the largest traditional smokie-curing company in Arbroath. Auchmithie was also unusual amongst other fishing villages of that coast in its setting of the fisher-houses high on the edge of a cliff above the harbour several hundred feet below.

The fish were originally smoked over domestic fires, but the need for more smoking facilities caused numerous 'smoke-pits' to be set up in half whisky barrels tucked into ledges on the cliff face. Making good use of the natural upward draught to keep the fires going, the fish, after being salted and dried, were hung in pairs on poles across the top of the barrels. The whole contraption was then covered with several layers of hessian sacking which was used to regulate the heat: on dry days with a brisk wind, more layers would be piled on to prevent the fire getting too hot, on wet, windless days the layers would be fewer. Originally, all kinds of surplus fish were smoked in this way but haddock became the most popular. In the early 1800s, a number of Auchmithie fisher-folk settled in Arbroath nearby. They built square, brick smoke-pits in their back gardens, continuing to make the smokie cure. By the end of the century, output from Arbroath greatly exceeded that from Auchmithie and the name of the smokie was changed to reflect this.

Today, the people of Arbroath continue to smoke in their backyards, selling smokies from small shop counters. When the pits are in use, the smell wafting through the streets is over-whelming. Though some prefer to remain small with a single smoke-pit, selling to loyal and regular customers, others have developed a more commercial operation in large plants. They have not, however, managed to reproduce the genuine smokie in computer-operated, high-tech kilns. Those who produce the original continue to work with the old method of small pits covered with sacking. Undoubtedly the best flavour is when the fish is 'hot off the barrel'. Otherwise, it may be split open and the bone removed, the centre filled with butter, and heated in the oven or under a grill. It has been granted Protected Geographical Indication (PGI).

TECHNIQUE:

The fish are gutted, beheaded and dry-salted for about 2 hours, depending on size, to draw excess moisture from the skin and impart a mild salty flavour. They are tied in pairs and hung over wooden rods; the salt is washed off and they are left to dry for about 5 hours to harden the skins. The rods are placed in the smoke-pit and hot-smoked over oak or beech, covered with layers of hessian. Smoking time is approximately 45 minutes.

REGION OF PRODUCTION:
EAST SCOTLAND, ARBROATH (TAYSIDE).

Finnan Haddock

DESCRIPTION:

A WHOLE HADDOCK, WITH THE HEAD REMOVED BUT THE BONE LEFT IN, SPLIT, BRINED AND SMOKED. COLOUR: PALE STRAW THROUGH TO GOLDEN BROWN; NO ARTIFICIAL DYE IS USED. FLAVOUR: LIGHTLY SALTED, DELICATELY SMOKED.

HISTORY:

A salt-cured haddock, known as a spelding, can be traced back to the sixteenth century when they are mentioned in the household book of King James V. They are also mentioned by Robert Fergusson in his poem *The Leith Races* (1773), 'Guid speldins, fa will buy'. In the same year, James Boswell describes them in his diary as, 'salted and dried in a particular manner, being dipped in the sea and dried in the sun, and eaten by the Scots by way of a relish'. He also says they were available in London. Speldings, however, were heavily salted and the subsequent move towards a lightly salted, smoked haddock began as communications improved and fish which might otherwise spoil could be delivered with enough dispatch. Due to the reputation of curers who smoked, as well as salted, fish in the village of Findon a few miles south of Aberdeen, the cured fish became known as a Finnan. It is also said that their reputation spread quickly through the country because they were transported to a dealer in Edinburgh by a relation who was guard on the Aberdeen to Edinburgh stage-coach at the beginning of the nineteenth century (Dyson, 1977).

They are mentioned by Robert Southey in his *Journal of a Tour in Scotland* (1819): 'A good breakfast as usual in Scotland, with Findon Haddocks, eggs, sweetmeats, and honey.' Included in the fishwife's creel of smoked and fresh fish, they were hawked about the country during the heyday of the East-coast fisheries and became common fare, cooked simply in milk and butter or made into the fishwife's soup-stew, admired throughout the country as a Cullen Skink. The reputation of Finnan haddock suffered in the 1870s when the cure was spoiled by the use of bad peat and a resinous, soft-wood sawdust, making the fillets acrid. It recovered its celebrity and quality, though not without competition from alternative modern cures using artificial dyes, 'painted ladies'. Sometimes described as a 'Golden' fillet, the lightly brined and lightly smoked skinless haddock or whiting should not be confused with the Finnan. A variation with more integrity is the undyed Aberdeen fillet, or smoked fillet, which can be used in the same way as the bone-in Finnan.

TECHNIQUE:

The original Finnans were split with the bone on the left-hand side of the fish, looking at the cut surface with the tail downwards. They were dry-salted overnight and smoked over soft 'grey' peat for 8–9 hours then cooled and washed in warm salted water. Other original Finnan cures around the country included Eyemouth and Glasgow 'Pale' which was a much milder paler cure, smoked for only 30 minutes to 2 hours and split with the bone on the right-hand side. A Moray Firth Finnan was split like a 'Pale' but smoked for about 12 hours making it a much darker, more heavily smoked fish. Methods today vary from commercially produced large-scale smoking in Torry kilns to small independent smokers, using simpler equipment.

REGION OF PRODUCTION:

NORTH EAST AND CENTRAL SCOTLAND.

Smelt

DESCRIPTION:

A FISH WITH A LIGHT OLIVE-GREEN BACK, SILVER STRIPE ALONG THE SIDE, AND A CREAMY WHITE BELLY; IT GROWS UP TO 20CM LONG, AND THE SOFT-TEXTURED FLESH IS SAID TO SMELL OF CUCUMBER OR VIOLETS – REASON FOR THE ALTERNATE NAMES OF CUCUMBER FISH AND CHERRY OF THE TAY.

HISTORY:

Smelts (*Osmerus eperlanus*) have always been considered a delicacy, and there are records of their fishery in various British rivers. Relatively little is known about the species, but they are an inshore fish, associated with specific rivers and estuaries which they enter to spawn. The River Tay has been noted for a reliable population of smelts for as long as people can remember and supports a very small commercial fishery.

According to the *Dundee Courier and Advertiser*, smelts were 'once a very popular meal in towns and villages around the Tay, dating back to medieval times when the fish was caught by the monks from the monastery at Newburgh'. Oral tradition, recounted by Sandy Doig, the person who currently exploits this fishery, states that around 1939–45, 17 yawls fished regularly for smelts. The number declined progressively in the intervening years until only one was left. This belonged to Charlie Johnston of Newburgh, who began fishing after the war, and continued up until his death in the early 1990s. The work is now continued by one boat from Newburgh; recently, others have shown an interest.

Smelts are usually fried, although they can be poached or pickled. They are also excellent smoked. In French, the fish is known as *éperlan*, translated by francophile Scots into sparling.

TECHNIQUE:

Smelts tolerate water of low salinity and, in the River Tay, the fishing ground is a 30km stretch of brackish water between Newburgh and Dundee. The fish travel up the tideway in autumn to spawn at the

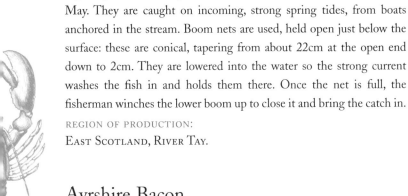

highest point reached by the tide and then return to the sea in April or May. They are caught on incoming, strong spring tides, from boats anchored in the stream. Boom nets are used, held open just below the surface: these are conical, tapering from about 22cm at the open end down to 2cm. They are lowered into the water so the strong current washes the fish in and holds them there. Once the net is full, the fisherman winches the lower boom up to close it and bring the catch in.

REGION OF PRODUCTION:
EAST SCOTLAND, RIVER TAY.

Ayrshire Bacon

DESCRIPTION:
SMOKED OR UNSMOKED CURED PORK FOR COOKING. COLOUR: CREAM FAT, DARK PINK FLESH. FLAVOUR: MILDLY CURED, VERY LIGHTLY SALTED; DEPENDS FOR ITS FLAVOUR ON THE BREED AND QUALITY OF PIG AS WELL AS THE CURE. AYRSHIRE BACON IS MADE FROM GREAT WHITE PREMIUM-GRADE PIGS. BOTH SKIN AND BONES ARE REMOVED BEFORE CURING. THE BACK OR CUTLET PART AND THE STREAKY OR FLANK ARE NOT SEPARATED. ONCE CURED, THE MIDDLE IS ROLLED TIGHTLY, THE FAT SIDE OUTERMOST. THE GIGOT (LEG) IS ROLLED AND TIED AND THE SHOULDER CUT INTO BOILING JOINTS. THESE ARE KNOWN AS AN AYRSHIRE ROLL.

HISTORY:
This is the only distinctive bacon cure in Scotland. It is thought to have arisen in the South-West, which has a history of dairying going back at least to the 1600s. In Britain, by-products from the cheese and butter industries have always been used to feed pigs. Potatoes too, grown in south-west Scotland, contributed much to their diet (Mabey, 1978). Demand may have been stimulated by the presence of many large, wealthy households in the Upper Clyde. Ramsay's of Carluke has been making Ayrshire bacon since 1857 and is now the largest producer.

The bacon was always skinned, boned and rolled. Rolling is necessary because the flank is left attached to the side, giving a very long rasher: the only sensible method for dealing with it is to roll the meat. In contrast to other cures in Britain, the carcasses are not scalded after slaughter. This is because the bristles, normally scraped away with hot water, are removed with the skin. The end product has a finer colour and firmer texture than meat which has been scalded.

The rolled back-bacon is usually cut thinly into rashers and grilled or fried. The round shape of the cut is convenient as a filling for a roll. In the cities of central Scotland, bacon rolls are a popular fast-food – eaten at any time of the day. The gigot is usually cut into steaks for grilling or frying. Both the gigot and the shoulder may be cut into joints for boiling. The term ham in Scotland loosely refers to any kind of bacon and not just the cured leg joint which is the usual English interpretation. In Scotland, this is called cooked ham or gammon.

TECHNIQUE:

Only gilts (young female pigs) of a specified weight are used by Ramsay's. The whole side is boned out and the skin removed. It is wet-brined for 2 days with a small proportion of nitrates for preservation. It is dried for 2–3 weeks before it is cut up and rolled. Some of the production is lightly smoked over oak chips. Some bacon with the back and streaky still in one piece, which has been cured with the skin on and the bone still in, is subsequently skinned, boned and rolled into the Ayrshire cylindrical shape. It is described as Ayrshire-style bacon but is not true Ayrshire. Some Ayrshire bacon curers also cure whole legs on the bone but because the skin and bones have not been removed, neither is this regarded as an authentic Ayrshire cure. The demand for smoked or unsmoked is a local preference. A special spiced cure is made for festive occasions, in small quantities to order.

REGION OF PRODUCTION:

SOUTH WEST SCOTLAND.

Cheviot Sheep

DESCRIPTION:

AS WELL AS THE ORIGINAL CHEVIOT, TWO DISTINCT STRAINS ARE RECOGNISED: THE NORTH COUNTRY (IN NORTH ENGLAND AND WEST SCOTLAND) AND THE BRECKNOCK HILL OR SENNYBRIDGE (IN CENTRAL WALES). CARCASSES (DRESSED WEIGHT, IN LATE WINTER) ARE 17–22KG (CHEVIOTS), 25–30KG (NORTH COUNTRY CHEVIOTS). GOOD MEAT CONFORMATION WITH STRONG SHOULDERS AND BROAD BACKS; CHEVIOTS ARE SMALLER AND BLOCKIER THAN THE LARGE NORTH COUNTRY CHEVIOT. LARGE, MEATY SHEEP WHICH YIELD WELL-FLAVOURED LAMB.

HISTORY:

The breed takes its name from the hills that run along the Scottish border. The primitive 'dun faced' sheep of the Highlands, noticed in the seventeenth century, was probably an ancestor. The breed we know today developed in the Northumberland-Berwick region (Hall & Clutton-Brock, 1989). Lincoln rams were used to improve the strain in the mid-eighteenth century, and some Leicester blood at the start of the nineteenth. Cheviots had some reputation by the time Mrs Beeton (1861) commented on them as providers of wool and meat. The breed society was founded at the end of the 1800s.

Not long before that, Cheviots were taken south and were found to do well on the high ground and in the exposed climate of central Wales. They were also taken north to graze the great tracts of land available after the Highland Clearances. With some Merino blood, these developed into a breed known as North Country Cheviots, or 'Northies'. A breed society for these was established in 1912.

Cheviot breeds are used for the production of quality lamb. A first cross is made with Leicester rams, and the female progeny is put to Suffolk, Downland or continental rams to breed large, lean, fast-maturing lambs. Much of this reaches the market as 'Scottish Lamb'.

TECHNIQUE:

All Cheviot breeds are hardy; the original is still the best for the bleak

hills themselves, which rise to 1,000 metres, with short grass and little cover for sheep. They live out all year. Extra feed, usually hay, is only given during the severest conditions and to pregnant ewes in the 6 weeks before lambing in mid-April. Hill lambs are late-maturing; they are killed for meat from August onwards but many are kept as stores on low ground, fed on arable crops and slaughtered in late winter.

The North Country Cheviot has two further strains. One is the Caithness, which, while living further north than the original Cheviot, is not as hardy; it grazes the low ground and rich grass of Caithness. The second is the 'Heather' or Sutherland, an exceptionally hardy, but somewhat smaller, sheep which does well in the harsh climate of western Scotland on unimproved native hill pasture and heather. Cheviot and North Country ewes are much sought by breeders for their excellent mothering qualities. Hill ewes are often sold at about 6 years to lowland farms, where they can be used productively for several more years in a gentler climate.

REGION OF PRODUCTION:
SCOTLAND; NORTH EAST ENGLAND.

Forfar Bridie

DESCRIPTION:

A HORSESHOE-SHAPED, BAKED BEEF AND ONION PASTY, WEIGHING 200–750G. COLOUR: PALE BROWN. FLAVOUR: SAVOURY BEEF AND ONIONS.

HISTORY:

Third-generation bridie-baker in Forfar, William McLaren, believes that his family's account of the origins of the bridie is more credible than the much-quoted story of Margaret Bridie of Glamis, renowned for her meat pasties which she sold in the Buttermarket in Forfar. According to McLaren, the bridie was a speciality of Jolly's bakery where his grandfather, James McLaren, served his time and learned to make them. This was in the late 1890s and meat was not commonly eaten by the majority of the population: the staple diet was based on porridge and brose, 3 times a day, Sundays and holidays included. Bridies were for special occasions, the horseshoe shape a lucky symbol eaten at the bride's meal, or wedding feast. The lucky bridie continues to be eaten at weddings, also christenings, but has now become a convenient everyday food.

Bridies in Forfar, made to the traditional method, have a high meat content which makes them more expensive than others made elsewhere. In the heart of Aberdeen-Angus country, people reckon lots of meat is essential to eating quality and are critical of any compromises. With a sausage-type filling and without onions, bridie has also become a generic name across Scotland for a crescent-shaped item made with puff pastry. This is not recognized in Forfar as authentic. They are eaten hot, for high tea or lunch with beans and bread and butter.

TECHNIQUE:

Jolly's nineteenth-century recipe (McNeill, 1929): 'Take a pound of the best steak. Beat it with the paste roller, then cut it into narrow strips, and again cut these into one-inch lengths and season with salt and pepper. Divide into three portions. Mince finely three ounces of suet. Make a stiff dough with flour, water and a seasoning of salt, and roll out thin into three ovals. Cover the half of each oval with meat; sprinkle with the suet and a little minced onion if desired. Wet the edges, fold over, and crimp with the finger and thumb. Nip a small hole on top of each. Bake for about half an hour in a quick oven and they will come out golden brown dappled beauties, fit for a king's supper.'

The modern recipe includes mincing the beef through a large plate to give a coarser texture than for pies, mixing with the other ingredients, then following the Jolly method of shaping the pastry and filling. Modern pastry recipes include a fat. Bridies are baked in a hot oven for about 40 minutes depending on size.

REGION OF PRODUCTION:

EAST SCOTLAND, FORFAR (TAYSIDE).

Galloway Cattle

DESCRIPTION:

AVERAGE LIVE WEIGHT FOR 16-MONTH STEER, 470KG. FLESH DEEPLY RED
WITH LIGHT MARBLING OF INTRA-MUSCULAR CREAM FAT. FLAVOUR AT
ITS BEST WHEN IT HAS BEEN HUNG 2–3 WEEKS.

HISTORY:

Though their subsequent bloodlines followed very different paths, the two modern Scottish breeds of black, hornless beef cattle – the Aberdeen-Angus and the Galloway – have superficial similarities which reflect descent from the same primitive stock. But while the first has responded to intensive feeding, resulting in a rapidly maturing animal, the Galloway has made the most of marginal and hill lands in the South-West of Scotland by producing a more slowly maturing breed.

During the eighteenth century, Galloway was a major source of store cattle which were taken by drovers to be fattened in Norfolk or Suffolk for the London market. By the mid-nineteenth, however, the droving trade had ended as beef breeds were developed for supplying Smithfield direct with carcass meat (see Aberdeen-Angus, p.73-5). South-Western cattle farmers, therefore, turned to dairying, and the beef cattle were forced to live in the hills.

The Galloway Cattle Society was formed in 1877 in Castle Douglas, still the headquarters of the breed. Until its inception, the polled Angus or Aberdeen cattle and the Galloways were entered in the same herd book, but with the founding of the society the copyright of the Galloway portion was purchased.

During World War II the value of the pure-bred Galloway for hill grazing was recognized and numbers were expanded with Government encouragement. While the breed has maintained its position, despite subsequent changes in Government policy, its most recent history has been significantly affected, once again, by its ability to forage on rough ground without too much expense, making it attractive at a time of rising costs. A variant is the Belted Galloway, so called for the vertical white stripe on its body.

Most Galloways are in southern Scotland with a concentration in the South-West; there are some in Cumbria and other parts of the North of England and a few elsewhere in England and Ireland.

TECHNIQUE:

The cattle are out-wintered and maintained on exposed hill and marginal land. They thrive and produce on low-cost rations in winter and in summer on unimproved rough grazing. They are particularly suited to extensive husbandry.

REGION OF PRODUCTION:

SOUTH WEST SCOTLAND.

Dundee Cake

DESCRIPTION:

A ROUND FRUIT CAKE, 180–230MM DIAMETER, 100MM DEEP (SOMETIMES OBLONG). COLOUR: DARK BROWN EXTERIOR, THE TOP COVERED WITH WHOLE ALMONDS, GOLDEN INSIDE, WITH SULTANAS. FLAVOUR: RICH, BUTTERY, FRUITY.

HISTORY:

It is claimed this cake originated as a by-product of the Keiller marmalade industry (see p.54-7). The firm was already working with Spanish and Mediterranean produce for orange marmalade; therefore the extra ingredients for the cake were not difficult to obtain. The habit of industrial food production was easily transferred from jam to cake. Until Keiller's was absorbed by a larger business in the 1980s, a gentlemen's agreement existed among the bakers of Dundee that only Keiller's should make the cake. However, this recipe, which appears indeed to have been developed sometime during 1850–1900, was widely copied by people beyond the city walls.

David Goodfellow, of the Dundee bakers, Goodfellow and Steven (established 1897), claims a direct connection with the early days of the Keiller version through a craftsman with first-hand knowledge from working in their bakery. He was reputed to have written down the specification before he went off to the First World War. This genuine Keiller item, as Goodfellow understands it, was a rich, buttery sultana cake, with no other fruits, no spices and certainly no cherries. The chief flavourings were the orange peel and almonds from Spain.

Recipes for Dundee cake have appeared in professional manuals for the last century or more. They have suggested variations (more often economies) on the simple richness of the original: topping with flaked, not whole, almonds, or adding black-jack colouring. Though more authentic cakes are now being produced in Scotland, the industry has not invariably maintained either the quality or the original concept.

TECHNIQUE:

Ingredients are slightly salted butter, muscovado sugar, eggs, plain cake flour, ground almonds, candied orange peel, sultanas, whole blanched almonds. These are mixed in the order given, save the whole almonds arranged on the top of the cake. It is baked at 180°C for 120–160 minutes.

REGION OF PRODUCTION:
SCOTLAND.

Glasgow Roll

DESCRIPTION:

A SQUARISH MORNING ROLL WITH HARD OUTER SURFACE, IOOMM LONG, 50MM HIGH. WEIGHT: 40G. COLOUR AND TEXTURE: FROM LIGHT BROWN THROUGH TO ALMOST BLACK ON THE SURFACE OF A BURNT ROLL; A LIGHT, OPEN, WELL-AERATED TEXTURE WHICH IS NONE THE LESS CHEWY. FLAVOUR: SALTY.

HISTORY:

This is a local form of the morning roll which developed its hard outer crust and airy, non-doughy, centre for the special purpose of holding bacon or a fried egg (or both at once) as a worker's breakfast. They were eaten in large quantities by men in places such as the Clydeside shipyards, as well as other local industries, as the midmorning snack. The roll was popular because of its robust quality. Alternative names were hard rolls and burnt rolls – so requested by those who liked their bread very well fired. Glasgow rolls are torn open rather than cut.

TECHNIQUE:

The dough is made with 100 per cent Canadian high-protein flour, mixed with water, liquid malt, yeast, and salt, and bulk fermented for 4–5 hours. Shaping is still done by hand, even in some large bakeries; final proving is also relatively extended. The rolls are baked for 14 minutes at 240°C.

REGION OF PRODUCTION:

CENTRAL SCOTLAND, GLASGOW.

Puggie Bun

DESCRIPTION:

AN OVAL BUN COMPOSED OF A FILLING OF GINGER DOUGH ENCLOSED IN A PALE CREAMY-GOLD PASTRY CASE WHICH IS SLASHED 4 TIMES ACROSS THE TOP; ABOUT 90MM LONG, 70MM WIDE, 15–25MM DEEP. FLAVOUR AND TEXTURE: DOUGHY, PASTRY DRY-TEXTURED; CRUMBLY, GINGER-FLAVOURED FILLING.

HISTORY:

The name is of unknown origin. The word 'puggie' or 'puggy', has several meanings in English and Scots dialects, including one relating to mixing operations and another (obsolete) a term of endearment. Whether either of these has anything to do with this bun is unclear. The alternative name of Gowrie bun, remembered by some older inhabitants in the south-eastern Scottish Highlands, suggests a strong connection with the lowlands along the north side of the River Tay, a fertile corn-growing area known as the Carse of Gowrie, near where these buns are still produced.

The puggie bun is an outer wrapping of plain pastry which hides a spiced and sweet filling which is almost equal quantities of treacle or syrup and flour. There are strong precedents for pastry-wrapped goods of this type in the baking traditions of the British Isles; the one which is most relevant in this context is probably the Scottish black bun, a large cake of dried fruit wrapped in pastry (see below). The filling for puggie buns is a substance called gundy dough by the bakers who make it (gundy is an old Scottish word for a spiced sweetmeat). It is a very similar mixture to one used for an old Scottish speciality, no longer made, which was a type of gingerbread called parleys, or parliament cakes. Kirkland (1907) comments that the dough for these 'was invariably made up in large quantities, and stocked in barrels, to be worked up afterwards as required'. Although these buns were apparently well known in central Scotland in the past, only one baker (in Cupar, Fife) has been located who produces them. He remarks that they are most popular with older people, who eat them as a snack or for tea, cut in half and spread with butter.

TECHNIQUE:

A gundy dough is made up from flour, syrup and spices and stored for use as needed. Pastry is made up fresh using a hot-water method and beef dripping as the fat. When required, the gundy dough is scaled off and shaped into balls; the pastry is wrapped around and sealed. The bun is turned so the join in the pastry is underneath and pinned or rolled further until the correct oval shape is achieved. The top is slashed. During baking the bun rises and the slashes open to reveal the filling; they are deliberately baked until rather dry. The gundy dough used to be raised with a mixture of pearlash and alum. At the turn of the century, bakers converted to bicarbonate of soda.

REGION OF PRODUCTION:
EAST CENTRAL SCOTLAND.

Selkirk Bannock

DESCRIPTION:

A WEIGHTY, ROUNDED BUN, FLAT ON THE BOTTOM AND CURVED ON TOP, 150–200MM DIAMETER, MADE IN SMALL AND LARGE SIZES. WEIGHT: 450G (SMALL)–800G (LARGE). COLOUR: GOLD. FLAVOUR: RICH BUTTERY YEAST BREAD FLAVOURED WITH SULTANAS.

The word bannock referred originally to a round, unleavened dough the size of a meat plate which was baked on the girdle and used by the oven-less Scots in place of yeast-raised, oven-baked bread. The word in Old Scots, *bannok,* is thought to come from Latin, probably through the influence of the Church and may have originally referred to Communion bread. It is now generally used to described any baked item which is large and round.

A Selkirk baker, Robbie Douglas, opened a shop on the Market Place in 1859 and so impressed his customers with the quality of his rich yeasted bannocks that in time they took the name of Selkirk. He discovered that the finished flavour was greatly influenced by the quality of the butter and, after some experimenting, found the best came from cows grazing on neighbouring pastures. He used only the best sultanas from Turkey and together with his baking skills produced the legendary bannock. On her visit to Sir Walter Scott's granddaughter at Abbotsford in 1867, Queen Victoria refused all else of the sumptuous baking save a slice of the Douglas bannock.

While a number of bakers now make the bannock, the original Douglas recipe is said to have come down from Alex Dalgetty, one of the bakers who worked with Douglas. Dalgetty's descendants continue to make the 'original' at their bakery in Galashiels, though Houston's in Hawick now owns the actual bakery where Douglas worked. Hossack's in Kelso has recently developed the Tweed Bannock using wholemeal flour.

Once an everyday bread dough, bakers now make up a special bannock dough. Some, but not all, continue to follow the original method of a 'sponge' which leaves the dough overnight for slower fermentation and development of a finer, more mature flavour.

TECHNIQUE:

Yeast dough is made up with about 4 parts flour to 1 part butter and lard. It is left to rise and then knocked back with 1 part sugar and 2 parts sultanas added.

'…bannocks and a share of cheese
Will make a breakfast that a laird might please.'
ALLAN RAMSAY, 'THE GENTLE SHEPHERD'

Softie

DESCRIPTION:

A ROUNDED BUN 100MM DIAMETER, 40MM HIGH. WEIGHT: 50–60G. COLOUR: GOLDEN. FLAVOUR: SLIGHTLY SWEET.

HISTORY:

This bun appears to have taken its name mainly to distinguish it from the Aberdeen butterie or rowie (see p.89-90) and is also sold as a morning roll. The fact that the rowie is a harder, crisper product gave rise to the term softie. This, at least, is one interpretation. An alternative name was soft biscuit: a literal description of their quality and the word biscuit describing a small roll or cake – a similar usage may be found in Guernsey (David 1977) and in North America. Though there is no written evidence, an Aberdeenshire baker of over 50 years' experience has established that softies and rowies have been common since the early 1900s. Production has spread beyond Aberdeen, down the east coast and Fife to Edinburgh. Because they contain more sugar than baps or rowies, and less fat than rowies, they are most commonly eaten at tea or supper with preserves, but may also be used as an envelope for savoury fillings. Simon (1960) records their being toasted for rusks.

TECHNIQUE:

Softies contain double the sugar used in a bap. Otherwise, the doughs are similar.

REGION OF PRODUCTION:

EAST SCOTLAND.

Black Bun

DESCRIPTION:

COLOUR: VERY DARK CENTRE, ALMOST BLACK WITH SPICES, DRIED FRUITS AND BLACK TREACLE, ENCLOSED IN A SHORT-CRUST PASTRY. FLAVOUR: INTENSE FRUIT, SPICE AND ALCOHOL.

HISTORY:

Though inextricably linked with the Scots and Hogmanay, not all Scots regard this cake as an essential element of the festivities. It has no real following in the Highlands and Islands, nor in the North East. Their spiced, fruited speciality is a clootie dumpling (see p.131). According to Meg Dods (1826), the bun, which was originally made with bread dough enriched with spices, dried fruit, eggs and brandy and then wrapped in a plain layer of bread dough, was made by all the leading Edinburgh bakers in the run-up to Christmas. She says that it was exported in sizes of 'four, eight, ten, twelve, sixteen and more pounds' to the rest of Britain.

Although this item was originally described as a 'Plum Cake' in eighteenth-century recipes, it is claimed by McNeill (1929) to have been the original Scottish Twelfth Cake used at Twelfth Night celebrations. Around the first half of the nineteenth century, it seems to have been rechristened a 'Scotch Christmas Bun', retaining its style as an enriched and yeasted bread dough wrapped in an thin outer casing of plain dough. The description 'bun' may have been introduced to avoid confusion with the meaning which the Scots had for 'cake' as a hard biscuit, as in oat 'cakes'. The use of 'Christmas' as a further qualifier is also confusing since, post Reformation, the Protestant church in Scotland actually banned Christmas as a Catholic aberration. A possible explanation for the name and subsequent development may lie in its success as an export product to neighbours who delighted in richly spiced foods. It could almost be described as an English Christmas pudding in a crust. Another clue to its English, rather than Scottish, popularity, is its inclusion by Meg Dods among the English baking specialities rather than in the chapter on Scottish national dishes. Eventually, it had become so intensely spicy and fruity that the bread dough was abandoned, very little flour was added to the spice and fruit mixture, and the whole mixture was wrapped in a short pastry crust. It was described by Robert Louis Stevenson as 'a black substance inimical to life'. The last mention of a 'Scotch Christmas Bun' appears to be around 1914; by 1929 it is described as 'Black Bun', the name it has retained ever since.

The main spices used in the eighteenth century were cinnamon, nutmeg, cloves, and caraway, along with currants, lemon and orange peel and almonds, with French brandy for good measure. In the nineteenth century, raisins are included and ginger used instead of caraway. McNeill's recipe in 1929 omits nutmeg, uses ginger and adds Jamaica pepper (allspice) and black pepper. All Scottish bakers who make the bun have their own spice mix and flavours vary from strongly peppery to mildly cinnamony. Black treacle is a modern addition. Today, it is almost invariably served with a dram of whisky.

TECHNIQUE:
Spices and fruit are steeped in brandy for several days, mixed with flour and sometimes grated apple and black treacle. These are pressed into a cake or loaf tin which has been lined with short-crust pastry. It is baked slowly until the pastry is crisp and the filling set firm. It may be stored for months in an airtight container.

REGION OF PRODUCTION:
CENTRAL AND SOUTH SCOTLAND.

Border Tart

DESCRIPTION:
A ROUND OPEN TART 150MM DIAMETER, 20–30MM DEEP; SOMETIMES ICED WITH WHITE GLACÉ ICING, WITH A DARK, DRIED-FRUIT FILLING; ALTERNATIVELY, A RICH SPONGE WITHOUT THE ICING. FLAVOUR: SWEET, RICH WITH DRIED FRUIT, BUTTERY.

The modern Border tart is different from the original casing of yeast dough filled with a rich egg custard and flavoured with marzipan, almonds, lemon and orange peel and sultanas. Border bakers have developed their own, more economical versions. It is now also known as Eymouth tart and Ecclefechan butter tart.

Sophisticated tarts are thought to have developed in this part of Scotland as a result of the French connection before and immediately after the Act of Union in 1707. Contemporary recipe books show the degree of refinement of Scottish tarts (often described as 'flans') from which the modern Border tart appears to descend. Interpretation by modern bakers has meant styles vary widely. No two are identical. They range from something akin to a Bakewell tart with a rich almond sponge, but which usually includes dried fruit and nuts, to an intensely sweet spongeless filling of fruit, sugar, butter and egg.

TECHNIQUE:

Made with a short-crust pastry case, filled with dried fruit, sugar, melted butter and egg. Alternatively, a sponge-cake filling, including a proportion of ground nuts. When baked and cooled, it is often coated with white glacé icing.

REGION OF PRODUCTION:
SOUTH SCOTLAND, BORDERS.

Cumnock Tart

DESCRIPTION:

A DOUBLE-CRUST, INDIVIDUAL, SWEET, FRUIT TART 130MM LONG, 100MM WIDE, 30MM DEEP. WEIGHT: ABOUT 110G. COLOUR: SHINY, BROWNED-SUGAR SURFACE WITH LIGHTLY BURNT EDGES. FLAVOUR: FRUITY, SWEET WITH SAVOURY LARD PASTRY.

HISTORY:

This is a regional variation and development of the Scotch pie (a raised pie filled with mutton or beef). The sweet version, using apple or rhubarb, was created by an Ayrshire baker named Stoddart around 1920, using the same savoury lard pastry as the meat pies. The tart was made first in Cumnock (Strathclyde). The second-generation owner of Bradford's bakery in Glasgow, Hugh Bradford, learned to make it from his father who had been apprenticed to Mr Stoddart. The tart is made to the original recipe for the chain of bakery shops owned by Bradford's.

TECHNIQUE:

Each tart is made from an individual piece of dough which is pinned out by hand to form an oval bottom or base. This is filled with apple or rhubarb. Sugar is added and a thin oval lid placed on top. An edge or rim is formed using the thumb and forefinger while sealing the lid to the base. They are baked for 20–25 minutes. During baking, they are glazed twice with sugar syrup to produce a rich colour and sticky, shiny top.

REGION OF PRODUCTION:
CENTRAL SCOTLAND, GLASGOW.

Kirriemuir Gingerbread

DESCRIPTION:

LIGHT-TEXTURED, CAKE OR DUMPLING GINGERBREAD, 120MM SQUARE. WEIGHT: 320G. COLOUR: DARK BROWN. FLAVOUR: SWEET-MALTED, LIGHTLY SPICED.

HISTORY:

The style of what is known today as gingerbread has changed from the original biscuit form, made with bread crumbs mixed with honey and ginger, rolled out flat, often stuck with whole cloves and baked until very hard. This had developed from the popularity of ginger throughout the country. No annual fair was complete without its gingerbread booth, the hard biscuit appearing in many novel shapes. It was the start of a tradition which survives in the wide variety of ginger-flavoured delights, both hard biscuits and soft cakes, such as parkin biscuits, wigs, ginger nuts, ginger snaps, coburg cakes, cracknels, fairings, honey cakes, Grasmere gingerbread and Yorkshire parkin.

The old hard gingerbread was known in Edinburgh as Parliament cake, described in Chambers' *Traditions of Edinburgh* (1868). The judges, lawyers and the men of Parliament Square would meet for their midday break of whisky, rum or brandy, accompanied by a salver of ginger biscuits or parlies. Very strongly ginger-flavoured, to match the strong drink, the recipe appears in Meg Dods (1826): 'With two pounds of the best flour dried, mix thoroughly one pound of good brown sugar and a quarter-pound of ground ginger. Melt a pound of fresh butter, add to it one of treacle, boil this, and pour it on the flour; work up the paste as hot as your hands will bear it, and roll it out in very large cakes, the sixth of an inch thick or less; mark it in squares with a knife or paper-cutter, and fire in a slow oven. Separate the squares while soft, and they will soon get crisp.'

While parlies are no longer made, Scottish bakers continue the gingerbread tradition with a number of other items, among them the soft cake known as a Kirriemuir gingerbread. It was first made by Walter Burnett, a Kirriemuir baker who sold the recipe to a plant bakery in East Kilbride in the early 1940s. It was made there until 1977 when the recipe was bought by the present owners of the recipe, Bell's of Shotts.

TECHNIQUE:

Like many British gingerbreads, the Kirriemuir involves syrup, an ingredient which probably replaced the honey of earlier recipes and has a similar humectant effect. The commercial product lists as its ingredients wheat flour, sugar, syrup, vegetable and animal fats, currants, malt extract, baking powder, spices, colour caramel, honey, preservative (E200). These are mixed with milk, and beaten to aerate (although chemical leavening is also added). They are baked at 160°C for 55 minutes.

REGION OF PRODUCTION:

CENTRAL SCOTLAND, LANARKSHIRE.

Parkin Biscuit

DESCRIPTION:

PARKIN BISCUITS ARE CIRCULAR, THEIR FORM RANGES FROM THICK, BISCUIT-LIKE CAKES ABOUT 140MM DIAMETER, 30MM THICK, TO THIN, HARD BISCUITS ABOUT 60MM DIAMETER, 5MM THICK. COLOUR: LIGHT GINGER-BROWN. FLAVOUR: SWEET, WITH GINGER.

HISTORY:

Parkin, known as perkin in Northumberland and southern Scotland, is the northern form of gingerbread. It is based on oatmeal, the grain of the region, mixed with flour and syrup and flavoured with ginger. Two distinct types exist: a soft sponge, found mostly in Yorkshire, south Lancashire and neighbouring areas; and a harder biscuit which is made mostly in counties either side of the Scottish border, although it is also found in isolated pockets further south. Stead (1991) speculates that it is derived from an older, honey-sweetened oatbread. The name was in use some time before the 1730s, when it was cited in a Halifax (West Yorkshire) court case about stolen oatmeal.

Parkin and the related 'thar' cake were originally made on a griddle. The biscuits may be modern representatives of this older form, though now baked in conventional ovens. Like sponge parkins, the recipes have been altered to include white flour and Golden Syrup or molasses. Although best known in the Borders, they are to be found as far south as Haworth in Yorkshire where a hard, bannock-like shortbread has been made in the town for as long as any one can remember. Biscuit parkins made further south are usually softer and thicker, and the dough is moulded by hand into a large round which is rolled out to the correct thickness before baking.

Parkin is traditionally a food for the end of October and beginning of November, especially Bonfire Night (5 November). Biscuit parkin is sometimes rolled very thin and cut into human or animal shapes, pigs above all.

All parkin biscuits are based on oatmeal, wheat flour, ginger, Golden Syrup and fat, often lard or beef dripping. Cake crumbs are required by one recipe. The exact proportions are variable. A recipe from Westmorcland requires flour and medium oatmeal, fat, black treacle and sugar in the proportions 3:3:2:2:2. The fat and treacle are melted together, flour, ginger and bicarbonate of soda mixed in, oatmeal and sugar added. The dough is rolled out, cut into rounds and baked at 170°C for 30–40 minutes.

REGION OF PRODUCTION:

SCOTTISH BORDERS; NORTH ENGLAND.

Paving Stone

DESCRIPTION:

A LONG, NARROW BISCUIT, LIKE A CYLINDER CUT IN HALF LENGTHWAYS, ABOUT 70MM LONG, AND 20MM HIGH AT THE THICKEST POINT, TAPERING TOWARDS THE ENDS. COLOUR: MID-BROWN, CONTAINING CURRANTS, WITH SUGARY WHITE OUTER COATING. FLAVOUR AND TEXTURE: SPICY, QUITE SWEET, WITH AN AERATED, HARD TEXTURE WHICH SOFTENS A LITTLE ON KEEPING.

HISTORY:

The origin of these biscuits, a type of gingerbread, is unknown. Made in eastern Central Scotland, they appear to be the speciality of one company, which was founded in 1919, which has been making them ever since. Many recipes for crisp gingerbreads are to be found in Scotland. Edinburgh, not far to the south of Fife, was famous for its Parliament cakes (see Kirriemuir gingerbread, above). Parkins, hard gingerbread biscuits which soften on keeping, are also known in the South and East of Scotland. The coating of grained sugar given to Paving Stones seems to be unique in British cookery.

TECHNIQUE:

The exact method is a trade secret, but the biscuits call for a dough based on creamed fat and sugar, mixed with flour, spices, baking powder, currants and milk. After baking, boiled sugar is poured on to an oiled slab; the biscuits are placed on top and tossed, using wooden bats, until the sugar grains and forms a white coating on the biscuit surface. The biscuits are separated, cooled and dried.

REGION OF PRODUCTION:
EAST SCOTLAND, FIFE.

Raggy Biscuit

DESCRIPTION:
A CIRCULAR BISCUIT WITH AN IRREGULAR EDGE, 70MM DIAMETER, 5MM DEEP. COLOUR: CREAM TO LIGHT GOLD SURFACE, DARKER EDGES; IRREGULAR DOCKING IN A BAND ACROSS THE CENTRE OF THE BISCUIT. FLAVOUR AND TEXTURE: CRUNCHY, LIGHTLY SWEETENED.

HISTORY:
These are a type of plain biscuit, slightly shortened and sweetened, formerly popular in Scotland and related to numerous others once made in the British Isles. Eric Milne of Cupar (Fife), the only baker traced who now makes them, comments that at least one other town in the area, Brechin, made a similar product, known as heckle biscuits, which were plainer. Heckle is a local dialect word meaning to dock or to puncture the surface of the uncooked biscuit with a pattern of small holes to prevent blistering during cooking. He also remarks that they show similarities to Abernethy biscuits, another Scottish speciality with a history stretching back 200 years.

It seems possible that raggies represent the plain, hand-made biscuits from which the modern Abernethy developed: Kirkland (1931) commented on the popularity of hand-made Abernethies in Scotland and said that (although the recipe is different) they 'have the quality of eating very short – in fact, not unlike ordinary shortbread'. He also notes the dough had to stand for a long time before it was moulded into biscuits, otherwise they cracked all round the edges – an effect which is encouraged in raggy biscuits and has given them their name. Raggies are nowadays eaten with cheese.

The exact recipe and method are trade secrets. Ingredients are flour, a relatively low proportion of fat (lard is used for many plain biscuits in Scottish baking) and sugar. Recipes for old-fashioned biscuits of this type also call for water to mix, and some involve raising agents. After mixing, the dough is scaled off and pinned out by hand to give the characteristic rough, 'raggy' appearance, docked several times in the centre, and baked in a hot oven until golden and crisp.

EAST CENTRAL SCOTLAND.

Edinburgh Rock

STICKS 10–15MM DIAMETER, 120–140MM LONG. COLOURS AND FLAVOURS: THERE ARE 7 CUSTOMARY TYPES, WHITE (VANILLA), PINK (RASPBERRY, STRAWBERRY), GREEN (LIME), FAWN (GINGER), LEMON (YELLOW) AND ORANGE. COMPOSITION: SUGAR, WATER, COLOUR AND FLAVOURINGS. IT HAS A POWDERY, CRYSTALLIZED TEXTURE.

Edinburgh rock is said to have been discovered accidentally by a nineteenth-century Edin-burgh confectioner, Alexander Ferguson, popularly known as 'Sweetie Sandy'. He found some rock which had been left uncovered in the warm atmosphere of the sweet factory for several months. The rock had crystallized to a brittle texture and its pleasant crunch and delicate flavour became so popular that it was the foundation of Ferguson's business. He became one of Edinburgh's most successful confectioners.

However, the technique of pulling sugar and then allowing it to grain has been known for many centuries, and a mid-fifteenth-century sugar-boiling text of northern provenance, in archives held in the City of York, gives instructions for making 'penides', or sugar sticks. At the end of the recipe, the confectioner is told to leave them in a warm place to take the toughness off them (i.e. to allow them to soften by graining). Whether Ferguson rediscovered this or built on an older tradition is not clear. This rock is now made by many confectioners and is sold throughout the country.

In many sweets, the confectioner makes strenuous efforts to avoid 'graining' (recrystallization of the sugar once manufacture is complete). In Edinburgh rock, the reverse is true and graining is positively encouraged by omitting ingredients such as acids and adding seed crystals in the form of powdered sugar to the boiled mixture. A batch commences by mixing sugar and water, and boiling it to 130°C (hard ball); it is then poured on to a slab. The flavourings are added and the sugar is dusted with icing sugar and 'pulled' until it hardens, when it is set in the rock shape. The pieces of rock are coated in icing sugar and left in a warm atmosphere until the rock becomes powdery. This takes 1–7 days. Rock with added glucose is made by some but is not regarded as authentic as it produces a 'claggie' (sticky) texture.

REGION OF PRODUCTION:
SOUTH SCOTLAND.

Hawick Balls

DESCRIPTION:
ROUND BALLS, 20MM ACROSS. COLOUR: DARK BROWN. FLAVOUR: PEPPERMINT. COMPO-SITION: SUGAR, GLUCOSE, BUTTER, MINT ESSENCE, BURNT (CARAMELIZED) SUGAR.

HISTORY:
The remnants of a strong tradition of sugar-boiling by home confectioners, street hawkers and grocers in small towns in Lowland Scotland survive in a number of distinctive local and national sweets. Hawick balls, locally known as Taffy [toffy] Rock Bools [balls], are one

of these. The area in which they are made, the Scottish Borders, has a particularly rich selection of local sweet specialities, many of which are flavoured with mint.

Notable sweetie-makers Jessie McVitie and Aggie Lamb made them in their shop in Drumlanrig Square in Hawick around the 1850s. Another local maker was grocer John Hill, who put out a sign in the early 1900s advertising his 'Home Made Hawick Balls'. John Hill's son, David, carried on making them in the back shop until he died in 1978. The business was bought by a firm of local bakers who continued the name of the firm and its tradition, until they passed it on to a larger sweet manufacturer. Hawick balls are not toffee as it is now generally understood: a mixture of sugar cooked with dairy produce. Earlier use of the word taffy suggests they may once have been pulled sweets; or it may simply be applied to denote a high-boiled mixture of sugar, the sense of the word as used by modern confectioners.

TECHNIQUE:

A mixture of sugar, water, butter and glucose is boiled to 160°C (hard crack), then poured on an oiled slab. Peppermint flavouring is folded into the hot sugar, then a moulding machine shapes the round balls. They are packed in air-tight containers as soon as they have cooled.

REGION OF PRODUCTION:

SOUTH SCOTLAND, HAWICK (BORDERS).

Jeddart Snails

DESCRIPTION:

BOILED SWEETS, 20MM ACROSS, TWISTED ON CUTTING TO MAKE AN UNEVEN SNAIL-LIKE SHAPE. COLOUR: DARK BROWN. FLAVOUR: BUTTERY, MILDLY PEPPER-MINT. COMPOSITION: SUGAR, BUTTER, CREAM OF TARTAR, OIL OF PEPPERMINT.

HISTORY:

Sweet confectionery in Scotland dates back to the first shiploads of sugar from the West Indies which came up the Clyde in the late 1600s, giving rise to an important refining and sweet-boiling industry. While at one time a large range of sweeties was made by small confectioners and itinerant sugar-boilers, only a few have survived. The Borders region is particularly rich in local specialities.

'Jeddart' is the colloquial name for the town of Jedburgh, where the Snails are made. The recipe is said to have been brought to the Borders by a prisoner of war during the Napoleonic wars. Released to work for local people, he is reputed to have made the sweets for a family named Curl. The original recipe has been handed down from one generation to the next to the present owner, Bill Millar, who runs a greengrocer's in Jedburgh. Demand currently outstrips supply but the family is reluctant to expand, feeling that a larger factory-type operation would destroy the character of the sweetie.

TECHNIQUE:
These sweets are hand-made in back-of-shop, sweetie-boiling fashion; the family boils up 6–15lb (6kg) batches of sugar on 3 afternoons a week. The ingredients are boiled to hard crack (154°C), poured on to the table and worked by hand, that is, pulled into long sticks which are twisted and cut into the snail shape.

REGION OF PRODUCTION:
SOUTH SCOTLAND, JEDBURGH (BORDERS).

Moffat Toffee

DESCRIPTION:
A DARK BROWN SWEET WITH AN ASTRINGENT, SHERBET-LIKE CENTRE, MEASURING 125MM ACROSS.

HISTORY:
The enthusiasm for sugar confectionery in Scotland developed to a peak in the Victorian period as ships loaded with sugar from the West Indies sailed up the Clyde to be refined in Greenock, popularly known as 'Sugaropolis'.

Making a living from sweetie-boiling became a common occupation for many small traders. They would boil up a few pans of sugar in the back shop. Janet Keiller – of marmalade fame – is reputed to have used her sweetie-boiling pans to make her first marmalade. Though many of the colourful and unusual sweets hawked round the streets and markets have not survived the passing of their original makers, remnants of this tradition exist in a number of distinctive local confections.

The recipe for Moffat Toffee has been in Blair Blacklock's family for at least 3 generations. Its origins, however, have been lost and no more can be said than that Mr Blacklock remembers his great-grandmother making sweets. The toffee is largely sold in the family sweet shop in the centre of Moffat.

TECHNIQUE:

The sugar is boiled to 148°C (hard crack). Some of the mixture is poured onto a slab and worked or pulled on a pulling machine to aerate it and lighten the colour. It would appear that it is at this point that the 'secret' ingredient is added. This flavoured and lighter mixture is then encased in the original, and pulled into thin sticks which are cut into sweets.

REGION OF PRODUCTION:

SOUTH WEST SCOTLAND, MOFFAT (DUMFRIES AND GALLOWAY).

Starry Rock

DESCRIPTION:

STICKS, 120MM LONG, 70–100MM DIAMETER. WEIGHT: 15G. COLOUR: PALE YELLOW-GOLD. FLAVOUR: SWEET, SLIGHTLY LEMON.

HISTORY:

Starry Rock is an old-fashioned sweet of the same type as barley sugar. Recipes appear in many early manuals and it was probably widespread during the 1800s. In the small Scottish town of Kirriemuir, this sweet has been known as Starry Rock since 1833, when the shop which still sells it was established. The present owner says the recipe is always sold with the shop. Older people in the town remember with great affection 'Starry Annie', who could be seen making the rock in the front of the shop early last century.

TECHNIQUE:

A mixture of sugar, Golden Syrup, water and a little fat is boiled to a very high temperature; secret flavouring essence is added. The mixture is poured on a marble slab and worked a little, then pulled out by hand to make sticks and cut into appropriate lengths.

REGION OF PRODUCTION:

EASTERN SCOTLAND, KIRRIEMUIR (TAYSIDE).

Ginger Wine

DESCRIPTION:

LIGHT GREEN IN COLOUR, CLEAR TO THE EYE, SWEET AND DISTINCTLY GINGERY IN TASTE.

HISTORY:

In the late nineteenth century, *Law's Grocer's Manual* defined this as 'a British wine or liquor, generally made with water, sugar, lemon rinds, ginger, yeast, raisins, and frequently fortified with added spirit and a little capsicin'. Alcohols based on raisins, sugar and lemons fermented together had been known since the early 1700s. An early recipe for ginger wine appears in Mrs Raffald (1769); it is a sugar syrup flavoured with lemon and ginger, in which raisins were infused. Mrs Beeton (1861) gave a similar recipe, fortified with brandy after 2 weeks' fermentation. Among manufacturers, Stone's of London was especially famous. At the outset, the wine was made in the Finsbury distillery in North London (established 1740). It was sold by the cask, which shop-keepers bought and sold in parcels to their customers. One, Mr Stone, sold so much his name became identified with the product (Grigson, 1984). Though once there were many brands, only Stone's and Crabbie's now remain. Crabbie's, still working in Edinburgh, make 'green ginger wine'.

The recipes are trade secrets, but ginger wine is made from dried grapes steeped in water and fermented; powdered root ginger is added; the wine is filtered and matured for at least 9 months in large oak vats.

REGION OF PRODUCTION:
LOWLAND SCOTLAND, LONDON.

Scottish Cask-Conditioned Beer or Ale

DESCRIPTION:
SCOTTISH BEER IS GENERALLY REGARDED AS SWEETER THAN ENGLISH. COLOUR VARIES FROM LIGHT GOLDEN TO DARK BROWN. TRAQUAIR BREWERY IS THE ONLY BRITISH BREWERY TO FERMENT ITS TOTAL PRODUCTION IN OAK CASKS.

HISTORY:
The German method of brewing is thought to have been introduced to Scotland during the twelfth or thirteenth centuries. Ale derived from malted barley gradually superseded the original heather ale.

At this time, it was made in the monasteries all over the country until private citizens began to take over the monks' role as brewsters. For example, in 1495 the abbot and monks of Cupar granted the right of brewing to certain tenants. Ale remained the common beverage of Lowland and North-Eastern Scotland, including Orkney and Shetland, where (known as home-brew) it was brewed in every village tavern, as well as in the farmhouses, usually by the wives of publicans and farmers. The subject of Burns' poem, 'Scotch Drink', is not whisky but ale. These aproned brewers apparently thrived on their occupation, for the term brewster-wife was commonly used to describe any extremely stout woman. There a story that, in 1661, 'twelve brewster-wives, all of portly condition, ran a race to the top of Arthur's Seat for the prize of a cheese weighing one hundred pounds'.

A well which the monks of Holyrood in Edinburgh had sunk in the twelfth century was the source of water to brew their ale. It initiated what was destined to become one of the city's major industries. In 1600, the abbey had been abandoned and Holyrood was a royal residence. John Blair, an enterprising Edinburgh brewer, took over the monks' maltings at the foot of the Royal Mile, and started selling his beer to the palace.

As brewing was increasingly commercialized so the businesses and companies with which we are familiar today were established, centred on Edinburgh, Alloa and Glasgow. Some had won such a high reputation that exiled French royalists who took refuge in Edinburgh in 1831 called their liquor 'Scottish Burgundy'.

Edinburgh brewing owes much to a freak of nature in the form of a structural trough– a sort of underground lake – which runs beneath and beyond the Royal Mile from Fountainbridge to Arthur's Seat. It is this water that feeds the breweries along the line of the trough. It contains a high percentage of gypsum which is thought to constitute the flavour which has given Edinburgh ales their distinctive quality.

Brewing in Scotland has changed greatly since the Campaign for Real Ale (CAMRA) drew attention to the quality of those smaller breweries producing cask-conditioned ales and stouts. This includes a new version of the ancient Heather Ale, made using fresh shoots of wild heather and sold as 'Fraoch' (pronounced fruich, p. 354), as well as the oldest ale made at Traquair House at Innerleithen in the Borders, where ale was being brewed when Bonnie Prince Charlie sheltered during his stay in 1745. The twentieth-century laird, the late Peter Maxwell Stuart, set about renovating the brewery and revived the brewhouse using the original vessels. His heir, Catherine Maxwell Stuart, continues the tradition. Brewing now takes place twice a week to make the Traquair Ale. There is also a weaker brew known as Bear Ale. This was named after the famous Bear Gates at the entrance to the house. They were closed in 1745 after the Prince's visit. The family vowed never to re-open them until a Stuart king returned to the throne.

Hot water plus crushed malt is mixed in a mash tun, left for an hour, then drained through a sieve. It is transferred to a copper (hot-liquor tank), and brought to the boil. Some hops are added and the mixture boiled for 2 hours to reduce the gravity strength. The final hops are now added and the mixture boiled for 10–15 minutes. This is left to settle for 30 minutes, then transferred from the copper to a filter through a cooling system into the fermenting vessel. Yeast is added and left to ferment 2–4 days. The beer is cooled to 16°C, transferred to storage tanks and matures for 4–8 weeks after which it is bottled.

REGION OF PRODUCTION:
SOUTH SCOTLAND.

Irn-Bru

DESCRIPTION:

IRN-BRU IS ORANGE-GOLDEN IN COLOUR, ITS FLAVOUR SWEET-SPICY WITH A CITRUS TANG, RATHER LIKE BOILED SWEETS. IT CONTAINS AMMONIUM FERRIC CITRATE (0.002 PER CENT). THIS FORTIFICATION WITH IRON DISTINGUISHES IT FROM OTHER SOFT DRINKS.

HISTORY:

Prior to the development of twentieth-century medicines, herbalists made cordials and tonics, giving rise to a number of 'health' drinks. This tradition, combined with a strong temperance movement in the early decades of the twentieth century was a source of many patent bottled drinks made under brand names by various companies. 'Iron-Brew' was a common mixed-flavour drink developed in Scotland during the early 1900s and was made by several manufacturers, each with a different recipe. Few actually contained iron.

All these drinks were affected by changes brought about by World War II. Iron brews disappeared as the industry was rationalized and

'Dost thou think, because thou art virtuous, there shall be no more cakes and ale?'
WILLIAM SHAKESPEARE, *TWELFTH NIGHT*

companies became numbered production units. After the war, legislation was passed which made it compulsory to add 0.125g of iron per fluid ounce (30ml) to any beverage named iron-brew. There was also a rumour that the Government was planning to ban the misuse of terms like brew which did not actually apply to a brewing process. Because of this, and the fact that Barr's recipe did not contain the necessary amount of iron, in 1946 the then chairman of A.G. Barr decided to overcome the problem by registering the phonetic 'Irn-Bru' as a trade name. At the same time, a major advertising campaign with a cartoon strip depicting the adventures of 'Ba-Bru and Sandy' was inserted in one of Glasgow's main newspapers, the *Bulletin*, and ran until the 1970s. Other companies producing iron brews did not survive but Barr's Irn-Bru became so successful that it has now taken the title 'Scotland's other drink'. It is carried around the world by nostalgic Scots – particularly to football matches where Scotland's other drink is not allowed.

TECHNIQUE:

The flavourings that give these drinks their distinctive character are closely-guarded trade secrets. The ingredients for Irn-Bru are water, sugar, carbon dioxide, citric acid, flavourings, preservative (E211), caffeine, colours (E110, E124), ammonium ferric citrate (0.002 per cent). Manufacture follows the standard method for all carbonated drinks: the flavouring and colouring ingredients are mixed to make a syrup which is combined with water and sugar, carbonated and bottled.

REGION OF PRODUCTION:
CENTRAL SCOTLAND, GLASGOW.

Dundee Marmalade

DESCRIPTION:

COLOUR: BRIGHT ORANGE THROUGH TO DARK BROWN. COMPOSITION:
SEVILLE ORANGES AND SUGAR, SOMETIMES BLACK TREACLE OR BROWN

SUGAR. DUNDEE MARMALADE HAS SHREDDED PEEL. WHILE ONCE
PRESUMED TO BE MADE WITH ORANGES, MARMALADE IS NOW APPLIED
TO ANY CITRUS PRESERVE SUCH AS LIME, GRAPEFRUIT, SWEET ORANGE OR
TANGERINE. IT MAY BE FLAVOURED WITH BRANDY, WHISKY, GINGER OR
BLACK TREACLE.

HISTORY:

Today, nearly all bitter Seville oranges grown in southern Spain are
destined for marmalade for the British market. Pots of marmalade
have followed the British around the world for more than a century. In
the early 1900s, the Empress of Russia and the Queen of Greece,
granddaughters of Queen Victoria, had supplies sent regularly from
Wilkins of Tiptree. The firm of Frank Cooper of Oxford still has a tin
which was taken on Scott's expedition to the South Pole in 1911,
discovered in perfect condition in 1980. Marmalade has also been
taken by the British up Mount Everest.

In the course of its history, marmalade has generated at least a
couple of myths for which the Scots must accept some responsibility.
One involves the belief that it gets its name from Mary, Queen of
Scots. Another is that it was an invention of Janet Keiller, whose
Dundee family built the first marmalade factory in 1797. Marmalade
made its first appearance in both Scotland and England in wooden
boxes: a solid, sugary mass of *marmelos* (quinces), exported from
Portugal, and first mentioned as 'marmelada' in port records at the end
of the fifteenth century. This is what travelled with Mary Queen of
Scots when she became seasick on the crossing from Calais to
Scotland in 1561 and which may – or may not – have helped restore
her equilibrium. Quinces were regarded at the time as healing fruits.
Her request, 'Marmelade pour Marie malade,' was no more than a
medicinal pun.

The medicinal properties of oranges were also highly regarded.
Candied orange peel was eaten during a fast, so it was a natural thing
to pulp and sweeten oranges into a 'marmelade'. It first appears in
seventeenth-century English cookery books when it was eaten as a

sweetmeat to aid digestion. Now enter the Scots. Until about 1700, a bowl of ale with some toast floating in it had been regarded as the most warming way to start the day. Then came the tea revolution and thereafter tea and crisp toast was the meal *de rigueur*. If it was not to be floated or dunked, this toast required an accompaniment. A solution came in a bargain-load of bitter oranges from Spain, bought by Janet Keiller's husband from a boat in Dundee harbour. This she made into a preserve. According to her English recipe, you pounded and pulped, with much patience, with a pestle and mortar. Instead, she decided to use a French way which was quicker and which chopped the peel into shreds. With a shrewd eye to economy, she decided not to reduce this 'marmelade' to a concentrated paste but to make it less solid, which produced many more pots per pound. It was cooked for a shorter time, improving the flavour and making it easier to spread on toast.

The epicurean traveller, Bishop Richard Pococke (1704–65), indicates the use of what appears to have been marmalade for spreading on toast at breakfast: 'They always bring toasted bread, and besides, butter, honey and jelly of currants and preserved orange peel.'

TECHNIQUE:

In Mrs E. Cleland (1755) a recipe appears for shredded orange marmalade: 'To make a Marmalade of Oranges – Take your Oranges, grate them, cut them in quarters, take the skins off them, and take the pulp from the strings and seeds; put the skins in a pan of spring-water, boil them till they are very tender, then take them out of the water, and cut them and leave the thin slices to boil by themselves. To every pound of oranges put a pound of fine sugar, first wet the sugar in water, boil it a good while then put in half of the pulp, keep the other half for the sliced orange; to every mutchkin of the pulp you must put in a pound of sugar likeways, then put in the grated rind, boil till it is very clear, then put in Gallypots; when cold paper them.'

The fruit is softened by boiling on its own. It may be left whole or chopped before boiling. The pulp and water is measured and for every 500ml of pulp, 500g sugar is added. The pips are usually kept separate, but included in the boiling to aid setting, before the fruit is finely chopped. The marmalade is boiled until it sets. Seville oranges are harvested in January, and much marmalade is made at this time.

REGION OF PRODUCTION:
EASTERN SCOTLAND.

***

Also produced in South Scotland
TAYBERRY, TUMMELBERRY (P.105)
HEATHER ALE (P.95)
MEALIE PUDDING (P.75)
MUSSEL (P.64-5)
OATCAKE (P.92)
OYSTER (P.67)
SCALLOP (P67)
SPOOT (P.72-3)

North Scotland: North, West, & Highlands & Islands

Dulse

A BROAD-LEAVED SEAWEED WHICH GROWS TO ABOUT 30CM. THE YOUNG FRONDS ARE THIN AND PAPERY.; WEIGHT: SOLD IN 50G PACKS. COLOUR: A DEEP REDDISH PURPLE. FLAVOUR: STRONG, SALTY, IODINE AROMA AND FLAVOUR.

HISTORY:

In the Scottish Highlands and Islands, sea vegetables were originally a regular part of the diet; there are 22 Gaelic names for varieties of seaweed: that for dulse is *duileasg*. Gathered from the foreshore, dulse (*Rhodymenia palmata*) was used in broths, deepening the flavour with the seaweed's high content of strongly flavoured amino acids. Dulse was fed raw to children as an important source of vitamins in a harsh climate with limited resources. It was also sold in the nineteenth century along with tangle (*Laminaria digitata* or *saccherina*), in city markets by itinerant street-sellers to the cry of 'Dulse and Tangel'. Oral tradition states that seaweeds of various types were dried to preserve them. In recent years, there has been a revival of sea vegetables for their nutritional qualities and the unpolluted shores around the north of Scotland have begun to be exploited for their abundant seaweeds.

There are 2 variations on dulse: Autumn Dulse is harvested at that season, when the plant is more vibrant, the colour is deeper and the flavour more astringent; there is also Pepper Dulse (*Laurencia pinnatifida*) which is a variety of colours from red-brown to yellow-green and whose fronds measure up to 18cm. Long stems are chewed for their pungent flavour. Other harvested Scottish sea vegetables include dabberlocks, grockle, sugar ware, finger ware, and *sloke* (wild nori), which is laver in Wales.

TECHNIQUE:
Picking is direct from the sea bed by divers, who take particular care not to damage new growth. It is harvested just before it becomes fertile and builds up the bitter content which gives an unpleasant taste. It is air-dried in a recirculating drying oven at a low heat to preserve the flavour.

REGION OF PRODUCTION:
NORTH SCOTLAND.

Caboc Cheese

DESCRIPTION:
SOFT, DOUBLE-CREAM CHEESE ROLLED IN TOASTED PINHEAD OATMEAL TO MAKE LOGS ABOUT 10CM LONG, 4CM DIAMETER. WEIGHT: 125G. COLOUR: CREAM INSIDE, GREY OATMEAL OUTSIDE. FLAVOUR: RICH CREAM, BUTTERY WITH A MILD TANG.

HISTORY:
In the period prior to the Highland Clearances the native soft cheese of Viking and Pictish ancestry was made by every crofter with surplus milk. Its demise came with the increase in sheep farming and shooting estates, putting an end to the crofter's system of taking his cattle, sheep and goats to the mountain grazings in summer where the women and children made the peasant cheese known as crowdie (see p. 106).

A recipe for a richer cheese, made for the clan chiefs, is reputed to be the oldest historical record of a traditional Scottish cheese and was passed down through the female line of the descendants of Mariota de Ile, a daughter of a fifteenth-century Macdonald of the Isles. The present descendant, and owner of the recipe, Susanna Stone, has revived the cheese, making it in her creamery in Tain where she began by making the crofters' cheese, crowdie, in the early 1960s.

A pioneer of the post-war farmhouse cheese-making revival, she called the oatmeal-coated chieftain's cheese Caboc, a derivation from the Scots word for any round cheese 'kebbuck'. Others cheese-makers have copied the recipe with varying degrees of success and the cheese is now established in the Scottish speciality cheese market.

TECHNIQUE:
The recipe uses pasteurized milk from cattle on 3 designated farms. This soft, double-cream cheese is made with lactic acid but no rennet and the logs are finished by rolling in toasted pinhead oatmeal before packing. The exact method is a trade secret.

REGION OF PRODUCTION:
SCOTLAND, HIGHLANDS.

Orkney Farmhouse Cheese

DESCRIPTION:
A YOUNG, LIGHTLY PRESSED, UNPASTEURIZED COW'S MILK CHEESE. WEIGHT: 1–2KG. COLOUR: CREAM OR WHITE, YELLOWER WITH SUMMER MILK. FLAVOUR: BUTTERY, MELLOW. TEXTURE: CRUMBLING, SOMETIMES LIKENED TO SCRAMBLED EGGS.

HISTORY:
Because of their remoteness, farms on the islands of Orkney have continued the tradition of artisan cheese-making without interruption. Made on a very small scale, often with milk from only one cow, it continues for both family use and for selling locally. Only a small amount is exported to the mainland.

TECHNIQUE:
The milk is heated with rennet for about 15 minutes until it

separates. The curdled milk is hung in a muslin bag to drip for a day. It is mixed with salt and packed into muslin-lined moulds and pressed for 2–3 days, then unmoulded and matured in a cool draught for a few weeks, though it may be kept longer. The best cheese is made from May to October.

REGION OF PRODUCTION:
SCOTLAND, ORKNEY.

Air-Dried Salted Fish

DESCRIPTION:
HARD, DRY FISH, WHOLE OR SPLIT, WITH CREAM OR WHITE FLESH. FLAVOUR: SALTY, MATURE.

HISTORY:
Drying and salting the abundant fish from the seas off the North of Scotland was an important preservation process before refrigeration and rail transport. Various methods of curing white fish, for instance sillocks, cuiths, ling, cod and saith, gave distinctive flavours and 'our fisher-folk rely mainly upon the use of the elements to give them *goût*, such as sun drying, wind drying, exposure on the rocks within reach of sea-spray, and brief storage under turf' (McNeill, 1929). For long storage, excess landings were salted and dried on flat pebbles on beaches and hung up and air-dried on rows of hooks outside the houses until quite hard. This was especially true in the Shetlands where it was a staple of the winter and spring diet and where dried ling was a major export to Germany and Spain in the late 1700s (Hope, 1987). The export has continued and, in the 1950s, it was still being sent to the West Indies and Africa.

The habit of drying fish persists on both a domestic and commercial scale in some of the remoter parts of the mainland and on the Islands. Air-dried fish is also produced on the Orkney Islands and sometimes can be observed hanging outside on dry and breezy summer days. Air-drying is practised on a larger scale in

Aberdeen, and some fishmongers in urban areas of central Scotland produce small quantities of the cure.

In Scotland, cooking preserved fish normally meant boiling with potatoes, using the highly flavoured fish as a seasoning. Or the flaked fish was mixed with mashed potatoes to make a dish called hairy tatties, which was also formed into fish cakes and fried.

TECHNIQUE:
The fish are gutted and beheaded, then split if large, left whole if small. If large, the top part of the backbone is removed, then they are layered in coarse salt and completely covered. They may be left for a few days, or up to a fortnight, when they are removed from the salt. They may be washed and pressed (in some cases, between stones) to remove as much moisture as possible or simply hung up by the tails to dry, usually in pairs if they are small, in a cold place with a good draught until very hard.

REGION OF PRODUCTION:
NORTH SCOTLAND.

Kipper (Scottish Cure)

DESCRIPTION:
WEIGHT: UP TO 250G. COLOUR: PALE GOLDEN SKIN, LIGHT TO DARK BROWN FLESH. FLAVOUR: MILD SMOKE AND SALT.

HISTORY:
Though kippering herring was first developed in Northumberland in the 1840s, the Scots have a history of kippering salmon (see smoked salmon, p.115-6). The kippered herring's greatest misfortune was during the First World War, when food was in short supply. Some enterprising fish-smokers had the idea of feigning the kippering process. Reducing the smoking times and, therefore, reducing the amount of moisture lost, they dyed the fish a smoky colour, inventing the commercial coal tar dye Brown FK (for kippers).

Though generally regarded at the time as a good war effort, the habit persisted and it is only a small (but now growing) band of dedicated independent smokers who have kept true to the original concept of an undyed kipper. And now the large curers, who always resisted the move back to undyed fish, have taken to producing the original pale kipper as public concern about unnecessary additives and colourings in food has gathered momentum.

In Scotland independent smokers are concentrated around the West-coast grounds where plump herring, particularly from the Minch and Loch Fyne, have a history of quality. Undyed kippers were smoked in large sheds on the pier at Mallaig and the Mallaig kipper is classed, along with the Loch Fyne, as one of the best cures. The undyed Loch Fyne kipper is described by McNeill (1929): 'Some years ago, when staying at a fishing port on Lochfyneside, I used to watch the herring-boats sail in at dawn and unload their cargo, which was run straight up to the kippering sheds. Here the fish were plunged into a brine bath and thereafter hung up to smoke over smouldering oak chips, while their colour changed slowly from silver to burnished copper.'

TECHNIQUE:
Usually brined in salt for about 30 minutes to provide a shine rather than to impart a strong salt taste, they are then cold-smoked for 18–24 hours over oak chips (sometimes from whisky barrels). Individual curers have their own brining recipes with 'secret' flavourings.

REGION OF PRODUCTION:
WEST SCOTLAND.

Mussel (Scotland)

DESCRIPTION:
COMMON MUSSEL: 50–80MM LONG; HORSE MUSSEL: 150–200MM LONG.
COLOUR: BLUE-BLACK SHELLS, BRIGHT ORANGE FLESH.

HISTORY:
As part of the general foraging for seafood, both common mussels,

Mytilus edulis, and the large horse mussel, *Modiolus modiolus*, were eaten by Scottish peasants living in coastal areas. Mussel brose was a common dish, mentioned in a poem by Robert Fergusson (1750–74), and according to a traditional recipe (McNeill, 1929), it was made with cooked mussels and their liquor, fish stock and milk. These were poured on top of a handful of oatmeal in a bowl, as you do for a brose, and returned to the pan for a few minutes to cook through.

Mussels were also a common street food; fishwives are recorded setting up market stalls selling mussels in saucers, plus condiments. The tradition survives in The Barras street-market in Glasgow (the name deriving from a common stall, originally a simple barrow) where several shops sell plates of freshly cooked shellfish, mostly mussels, horse mussels and whelks. They may be sold either on the premises at a simple bench and table, when they are served with a cup of the bre (cooking liquor), or they may be sold as a takeaway in a paper bag.

TECHNIQUE:
While some mussels are collected wild, cultivation has been practised throughout Europe. First recorded in Scotland in the 1890s, several experiments took place on the east coast growing mussels on ropes but the idea was abandoned following a series of disasters. In 1966, however, experiments were resumed cultivating again on ropes and commercial ventures started in the early 1970s using ropes attached to both longlines and rafts. Both methods continue, with each farmer developing a system which suits his particular site. Once harvested they are washed and graded. Horse mussels are harvested from natural beds lying at extreme low water mark.

REGION OF PRODUCTION:
NORTH SCOTLAND AND GENERAL SCOTLAND.

Oyster (Scotland)

DESCRIPTION:

NATIVE OYSTERS ARE FAN-SHAPED, ALMOST CIRCULAR, ONE HALF OF THE SHELL IS FLAT, THE OTHER CUPPED. THE SHELL OF THE PACIFIC OYSTER IS MORE DEEPLY CUPPED, ROUGHER AND MORE ELONGATED. MOST WEST-COAST OYSTERS ARE PACIFIC. DIMENSIONS: GRADED BY SIZE 70–80G; 80–95G; 95G AND UPWARDS. COLOUR: A WIDE VARIETY OF COLOUR AND TEXTURE ACCORDING TO THEIR ORIGIN. FLAVOUR: SEA-TASTING, DETERMINED BY THE FEEDING AND VARIES FROM LOCH TO LOCH. IN TERMS OF THE QUALITY OF THE FLAVOUR, ALL SCOTTISH OYSTERS ARE GRADE A, THAT IS, THEY HAVE NOT BEEN PURIFIED BY PASSING THROUGH PURIFICATION TANKS OR HELD IN AERATED HOLDING TANKS BEFORE SALE.

HISTORY:

Eaten with great relish, oysters were celebrated during the heyday of the oyster cellars of Georgian and Victorian Edinburgh. They were consumed, nightly, by the thousand. The poet James Hogg (1770–1835), an enthusiast, complained that 'a month without an R has nae right being in the year'. So cheap and plentiful was the supply, that recipes for soups and stews often demanded 60 oysters. These were the large European native oysters which are mentioned by Martin Martin in his *Description of the Western Islands of Scotland* (1709) as growing on rocks and 'so big that they are cut in four pieces before they are ate'.

The beds of native oysters fell victim to pollution and over-fishing and by around 1950 were almost totally wiped out. Revival, which has occurred over the last 30 years, has depended entirely on farming gigas (*Crassostrea gigas*) – though some farms are experimenting with natives – in sheltered sea-lochs on the West coast, the Islands and in Orkney. The gigas has been used since cold water inhibits breeding. This means they do not retain their eggs and can therefore be sold all year without tasting unpleasant.

TECHNIQUE:

Lochs chosen for oyster farming must have shelter, total lack of pollution and a rich supply of nutrients. The most common methods are to put the young seed (brought from hatcheries at about 12–15mm) into mesh bags on metal or wooden trestles at low-water mark, or into plastic trays which are stacked on the sea bed or suspended from a headline. The first gives access to sort and grade during the spring tides and the second, weather permitting, allows work at any time. Allowing the oysters to be uncovered is considered important since it allows them to close tightly and survive in air, essential when they are eventually transported for sale. They are usually harvested after 2 summers' feeding.

REGION OF PRODUCTION:
WEST SCOTLAND AND GENERAL SCOTLAND.

Scallop (Scotland)

DESCRIPTION:
GREAT OR KING SCALLOP (*PECTEN MAXIMUS*): FLAT BOTTOM SHELL AND A CONCAVE UPPER SHELL; MUSCLE DIAMETER APPROXIMATELY 50MM; MINIMUM LEGAL CARAPACE SIZE 100MM. QUEEN SCALLOP (*CHLAMYS OPERCULARIA*): TOP AND BOTTOM SHELLS BOTH CONCAVE; MUSCLE DIAMETER APPROXIMATELY 30MM. PRINCESS SCALLOP (AN IMMATURE QUEEN): MUSCLE DIAMETER APPROXIMATELY 10MM. THE GREAT SCALLOP AND THE QUEEN HAVE BEIGE SHELLS, AND A CREAM OR WHITE MUSCLE SURROUNDED BY AN ORANGE ROE. THE PRINCESS SCALLOP HAS A REDDISH-PINK SHELL AND A CREAM OR WHITE MUSCLE BUT THE ROE, BECAUSE OF ITS AGE, HAS NOT DEVELOPED. THEY HAVE A DISTINCTIVE AND SUBTLE SEA-FLAVOUR FROM RICH FEEDING IN UNPOLLUTED NORTHERN WATERS.

HISTORY:
The food culture of the Western Highlands and Islands of Scotland was, among the impoverished peasantry, one of subsistence. It was not until the nineteenth century that commercial fisheries began to develop on this coast, under the influence of the British Fisheries

Society who established ports for processing and collection. The expansion of the railway network meant the catch could reach markets hitherto unattainable.

An important dredged and dived scallop industry arose in the 1950s and 1960s, harvesting from natural West-coast beds. Research into scallop farming began on the Isle of Man in the early 1970s and, although no farming takes place in that location, the methods developed have been successfully applied off the West coast of Scotland. The development of the farmed scallop began here in the 1974 and its popularity has grown, partly due to its guarantee of quality. The age of the farmed scallop is controlled to around 5 years, yielding tender muscle and regular size, encouraging wider use of farmed scallops in the catering industry.

TECHNIQUE:

Scallop farming produces a more uniform supply than wild scallops. The young spat are put into collectors where they attach themselves to the sides of the nets. As their shells begin to grow they fall off the nets and are gathered and put into free-floating 'lantern' nets suspended in the sea water where they feed and grow (queen scallops for 18 months to 2 years; king scallops for 4–5 years). Princess scallops are harvested when they are about 12 months old. Aquaculture is still a developing industry and methods are constantly undergoing change. Ranching, or bottom culture, is seen by some farmers as the way forward. This has always been a risky business because it was not possible to protect stocks from dredgers or divers. Recently, however, the first Several Fishery Order has been recommended to be granted to stocks of farmed scallops giving them legal protection.

REGION OF PRODUCTION:

WEST SCOTLAND AND GENERAL SCOTLAND.

Scotland suffers poor press when it comes to its eating habits, which is a real pity when you consider what incredible produce it has. I have always looked upon Scotland as a very rich larder of ingredients, from the most amazing beef and venison, to salmon, scallops and lobster. This was one of my signature dishes at Royal Hospital Road. Our customers protested every time we changed the menu so we've been offering it off-and-on for years. We insist on using diver-caught scallops (mostly from Western Scotland) at the restaurants – the dredged alternatives often end up terribly muddy or damaged and are simply not an option. For this dish, we generally use large king scallops, which we dust with a little bit of curry powder to enhance their natural sweetness.

Gordon Ramsay

CHEF, RESTAURANTEUR, BROADCASTER AND AUTHOR

Pan-roasted Scallops with Cauliflower Purée

Serves 4

12 LARGE SCALLOPS
1 TSP MILD CURRY POWDER
SEA SALT AND FRESHLY GROUND BLACK PEPPER
1 TBSP OLIVE OIL
A HANDFUL OF SALAD LEAVES (SUCH AS FRISÉE AND LAMBS
    LETTUCE), TO GARNISH

Vinaigrette:
1 TBSP SHERRY VINEGAR
3 TBSP OLIVE OIL
SEA SALT AND FRESHLY GROUND BLACK PEPPER

Cauliflower purée:
½ HEAD OF CAULIFLOWER (ABOUT 350G), TRIMMED
    AND CUT INTO FLORÊTS
30G BUTTER
1-2 TBSP MILK
100ML SINGLE CREAM
SEA SALT AND FRESHLY GROUND BLACK PEPPER

Shell, trim and clean the scallops, then pat dry with kitchen paper and chill them until ready to cook. Combine the curry powder with a teaspoon of salt and a grating of pepper and set aside. Mix together the ingredients for the vinaigrette and season to taste.

Trim the cauliflower and cut into florêts. Melt the butter in a saucepan and add the cauliflower. Sauté for about three-four minutes, add the milk and cream and partially cover the pan with a lid. Cook for another three-four minutes over gentle heat until the florêts are soft. Season well to taste. While still hot, tip the cauliflower and cream into a food processor and blend for a few minutes until really smooth, scraping the sides of the processor a few times.

Lightly sprinkle the curry powder mixture on both sides of the scallops. Heat a little oil in a large non-stick frying pan. Cook for just a minute on each side and turn them in the order they were put in. They should be nicely brown on both sides and feel springy when pressed. Remove from the pan and leave to rest for a minute. Slice each in half horizontally and lightly season again.

Place the six scallop halves on little spoonfuls of the cauliflower purée around each plate. Garnish with the salad leaves and drizzle with the vinaigrette to serve.

'He was a very valiant man who first ventured on eating of oysters.'
THOMAS FULLER, *THE HISTORY OF THE WORTHIES OF ENGLAND*

Spoot

DESCRIPTION:

A BIVALVE; THE NARROW SHELL CAN BE UP TO 12CM LONG BUT IS ONLY 1.5–2CM WIDE; IT IS STRAIGHT, AND SLIGHTLY GREEN-BROWN IN COLOUR. THE MEAT IS TRANSLUCENT WHITE, COARSELY TEXTURED, WITH AN EXCELLENT SEA FLAVOUR. IF OVERCOOKED, IT BECOMES CHEWY AND INEDIBLE.

HISTORY:

Spoots is the name in Orcadian dialect for *Ensis ensis*, the razor-shell clam. These are not eaten in the British Isles except by the inhabitants of some Scottish islands, who regard them as a delicacy. They form part of an ancient gathering tradition in an area in which food was often in short supply and all available edible items found use sooner or later. The Orkney Islands exhibit the strongest appetite for these fish. It is not clear for how many centuries they have been considered a local delicacy: the name spoots was noted by the beginning of the 1800s (*OED*).

The Moray Firth, a little further south, also yields spoots. Dived and dredged spoots are available October–May; hand-fishing takes place principally in March and September, when the equinox produces low ebb tides.

In the Orkneys, spoots are eaten for any main meal. They are taken plain, straight from the opened shell, or turned briefly in melted butter.

TECHNIQUE:

Spoots are renowned for being difficult to catch. They are found in wet sand, and are only exposed at very low ebb tides. The method for spooting is to walk backwards along the beach, watching for the little spoot (spout) of water ejected by these creatures, which lie concealed just below the surface. If one is located, the spooter inserts a knife into the sand to locate the shell and then twists it round very quickly to bring it to the surface. This requires practice and skill for if the spoots sense danger they burrow quickly downwards beyond reach. On some beaches, it is claimed that they can be brought to the surface by pouring a small quantity of dry salt into the hole on the surface, but mixed reports about the effectiveness of the technique are given by those who have tried. Modern methods in commercial use are diving (which also requires skill, as it too involves problems locating and catching the fish) and suction dredging, which is the easiest but the most capital-intensive method.

If desired, the fish can be left in sea water overnight to cleanse them. As spoots have shells which are permanently open at both ends, the risk of contamination is too great to allow them to be marketed alive like other bivalves; this may account for their localized popularity. Spoots are opened just before eating by placing the shellfish on a hot griddle and removing the meat as soon as the shells open. Or they can be placed in boiling water. The stomach bag can be cut away before consumption.

Although these clams are found on English beaches, they have not been gathered with any great gastronomic enthusiasm. An episode on the beaches of south Devon in 1998 left 200 holiday-makers lacerated on the feet by the (razor) sharp shells (hence the English name) that were unexpectedly exposed on the surface by abnormally low tides. No mention in news reports was made of their palatability, only their capacity to wound.

REGION OF PRODUCTION:
THROUGHOUT GENERAL SCOTLAND, HIGHLANDS AND ORKNEYS.

Aberdeen-Angus Cattle

DESCRIPTION:
AVERAGE CARCASS WEIGHT OF STEER AT 18–19 MONTHS, 275KG. FLESH DEEPLY RED, FAT CREAM-WHITE, MARBLED WITH INTRA-MUSCULAR FAT.

HISTORY:
Though the most widely known Scottish breed, Aberdeen-Angus is also the most recently established. Pioneer breeder Hugh Watson

(1780–1865), from Keillor near Dundee, first showed his black, polled cattle in 1820 and by 1829 was sending some of his stock from the Highland Show in Perth to Smithfield. Hitherto, cattle had been exported on the hoof for fattening in East Anglia. Now, the trade to London of prime beef in carcass (sending only the most expensive cuts) developed with the success of Watson's herd. This new method became the norm with the completion of the railway to London in 1850. Watson is regarded as having fixed the type of the new breed and by the time his herd was dispersed, in 1861, it had been highly selected within itself. For the 50 years of its existence, it seems he never bought a bull. He sold stock to William McCombie (1805–1880), of Tillyfour near Aberdeen, who carried on the programme, attaching the same importance to meeting the requirements of the London trade. The breed's main rival was Amos Cruickshank's Scotch Shorthorn, established in the 1830s when he and his brother became tenants of an Aberdeenshire farm. It could be fattened more rapidly, but did not milk so well and was less hardy than the Watson stock. To overcome its problems and to induce more rapid fattening in the Aberdeen-Angus, the characteristics of the breeds were combined. The Aberdeen-Angus cross Shorthorn became the source of most prime beef in Scotland.

The Polled Cattle Herd Book was started in 1862; the Aberdeen-Angus Cattle Society inaugurated in 1879. In 1891, a separate class at the Smithfield Show was provided for the breed and it has never lost its pre-eminence. At the Perth sales in 1963 a single bull made history with a world-record price of 60,000 guineas.

Changes have occurred in the last 30 years. A demand developed in the 1960s for a small, thick bull with a lot of meat. The trend reversed with entry to the EU, since which time the preference has been for taller, leaner animals with a minimum of fat. 'But this meat,' said the breed society president, 'does not have the succulence and flavour that the consumer requires. Thus the aim now is to have meat that has a marbling of fat through it, to give a healthy product that is succulent and tasty.' This has stimulated a new departure, as retailers themselves support the identification of beef as Aberdeen-Angus as a guarantee of quality. A Certification Trade Mark has been registered.

TECHNIQUE:

The breed thrives on low-quality pasture and rations such as silage and arable by-products. It converts these more effectively than most others into high-quality, early-maturing beef with marbled fat, making it both economically and environmentally desirable.

REGION OF PRODUCTION:
NORTH EAST SCOTLAND.

Mealie Pudding

DESCRIPTION:

A COOKED SUET AND CEREAL SAUSAGE IN SEVERAL SHAPES: A SINGLE LINK SAUSAGE, A SLICING SAUSAGE, A LARGE LINK SAUSAGE CURVED AND THE ENDS JOINED TO MAKE A LOOP, A BALL-LIKE HAGGIS SHAPE. WEIGHT: 125–250G. COLOUR: GREY. FLAVOUR: OATMEAL AND ONION, BUT DEPENDS LARGELY ON THE FLAVOUR OF THE SUET OR FAT.

HISTORY:

In the days before the turnip was used as winter feed for animals, Martinmas (11 November) was the time for killing the animals which could not be kept through the winter. 'Mairt' was an incredibly busy time and several families would join together to do the work. Every scrap of the beast was used – the meat salted and puddings made from the innards. Mealie puddings (black and white) were made when beef cattle were killed. In the original communal system, oatmeal, onions and beef suet were mixed with salt and pepper in a large basin. Then blood was added to some of the mixture to make the 'bleedy' ones (black puddings). The intestines were thoroughly washed, usually in a burn, and then stuffed loosely with the mixture. They were tied up and boiled in a large pot.

The operation has now become almost completely commercial,

carried out by either a butcher or meat-processing plant, though there are a few individuals who still make their own at home. They are consumed throughout the country. The pudding is sliced and fried with bacon and eggs; a whole pudding is cooked on top of a beef stew, or served as an accompaniment to meat or boiled potatoes; or they can be deep-fried and eaten with chips. They are also known as white pudding and, in Aberdeenshire as Jimmys while black puddings are known as Jocks. Without their skins, the mixture of oatmeal and onions is fried in a pan with fat and is known as 'skirlie' from the term 'skirl in the pan' meaning making a loud noise.

TECHNIQUE:

The 'Traditional Method' (McNeill, 1929): 'Toast two pounds of oatmeal in the oven, mix with it from a pound to a pound and a half of good beef suet and three or four fair-sized onions, all finely chopped. Add about a tablespoonful of salt and half that quantity of Jamaica pepper. Prepare your tripe skins as for Black Puddings and fill, not too full with the oatmeal mixture in the manner there indicated. Boil for an hour, pricking them occasionally with a fork to prevent them from bursting. These puddings will keep good for months if hung up and kept dry, or better, if kept buried in oatmeal in the girnel or meal chest.'

REGION OF PRODUCTION:
THROUGHOUT GENERAL SCOTLAND.

North Ronaldsay Sheep

DESCRIPTION:
SMALL, FINE-BONED ANIMALS, WITH DARK, TENDER, FINE-GRAINED, WELL-FLAVOURED AND SLIGHTLY GAMY FLESH. PRIMITIVE SHEEP HAVE A LOWER PROPORTION OF SATURATED FATTY ACIDS THAN COMMERCIAL BREEDS.

HISTORY:
North Ronaldsay sheep evolved in an oceanic climate, windy and wet

but mild, thanks to the Gulf Stream. The Orkneys are flat and low-lying; the soil is good and much is cultivated or used as pasture for cattle and sheep, which are part of a subsistence economy known as crofting. This incorporates small-scale farming and cultivation of crops like potatoes and kale, backed up by fishing and cottage industries such as weaving or knitting. All the good land is used for crops and cattle; sheep are expected to live on the common, less fertile land, which in the Orkneys often means the foreshore surrounding habitable land.

The first recorded comments on the native sheep were in the early nineteenth century (*OED*). In 1861, Mrs Beeton remarked they were 'restless and unprofitable'. They may be considered as ancestors of the Shetlands which, together with other primitive breeds found on the Scottish islands, probably owe many of their characteristics to introductions by the Vikings. The sheep now survive only on a single inhabited island, North Ronaldsay, and on several small holms or uninhabited islands the most notable of which is Linga Holm – hence their other names of Holme sheep or Holmies. In the early nineteenth century, a wall was built around North Ronaldsay's agricultural acreage to exclude these near-feral sheep from more conventional grazing. They have since lived on the foreshore, surviving largely on seaweed. They are physiologically adapted to this diet, utilizing dietary copper very efficiently, even developing copper poisoning on richer grazing. The ewes are brought into grass fields for a few weeks around lambing in May.

After long decline, the primitive breeds are now valuable for both genetic and commercial reasons. In the 1970s, fears for the health of this small population in so restricted an area led to the purchase of Linga Holm by the Rare Breeds Survival Trust who established and manage a flock there. There is a demand for their meat. However, the potential market is very distant, adding to difficulties and cost. Lamb from North Ronaldsay is available on the Orkneys and in a few specialist butchers on the mainland in late August and early

September. Other lambs are raised on the Orkneys to a more settled agricultural pattern: these are Cheviots (p. 25).

TECHNIQUE:

North Ronaldsay sheep are recognized to be exceptionally hardy and prolific. Meat from all the primitive breeds requires hanging for 7 days to develop optimum flavour and tenderness.

REGION OF PRODUCTION:

ORKNEY ISLANDS.

Red Deer Venison

DESCRIPTION:

A STAG WEIGHS APPROXIMATELY 105KG, HIND 70KG (CLEANED). THE MEAT IS DARK CRIMSON RED, CLOSE-GRAINED, WITH FIRM, WHITE FAT.

HISTORY:

The word venison formerly referred to the flesh of game in general. Now it is restricted to that of the various species of deer found in Britain. There is much early evidence for its use as food by the whole population. After 1066, first in England and later in Scotland, landowners became increasingly restrictive about hunting. In the Scottish Highlands, venison was caught and distributed through the clan, which shared equitably the produce of the land among its people. The deer were hunted by a method known as the tinchel (Hope, 1987). This involved a large number of men moving herds from the hills over days, or weeks, into a funnel-like enclosure at the head of a glen. The deer were killed as they attempted to escape. The animals concerned would be red deer, as the woodland species live on lower ground. This method was used into the 1700s. Thereafter, as landowners claimed the Highlands for themselves, the meat only entered the diet of the poor when it was poached.

By the nineteenth century the range of red deer had become restricted to very specific areas of Britain, by far the most important was the Scottish Highlands. At this time, the art of stalking, still practised today, became important. The factors which led to its development were the retreat of the deer to remote and inaccessible areas; the depopulation of the Highlands, reducing the manpower available; the availability of improved firearms; and the need for Scottish landowners to earn money – which they did by creating shooting estates. In 1811 there were 6 of these in the Scottish Highlands; by 1842, there were 40.

The pattern thus set has never been completely reversed and venison remains a luxury meat. For a long period in the second half of the twentieth century a large percentage of Highland venison was exported, principally to Germany. But largely due to several companies' efforts to reverse this trend, as well as the production of a small amount of farmed venison's unique flavour and high-quality, lean meat is now gaining more local customers.

The history of English venison is not so very different from the experience of Scotland. The meat of the roe deer and other species has always been jealously reserved to those groups who have had the privilege of hunting it: at first the king, then his noble vassals, then land-owners whoever they may be. Venison entered the general diet through gift, not sale, unless it was poached (Thompson, 1975). Culinary treatment of the meat has been conservative, but with better hanging and butchering techniques, as well as more available information, it is being used in a more adventurous fashion.

TECHNIQUE:

The season in Scotland is 21 October–15 February for hinds; 1 July–20 October for stags. After shooting, the deer are gralloched (innards removed) imme-diately. They are transported on hill-ponies to a collection point to be trucked in refrigerated vehicles to a production unit. Here they are skinned, inspected by a veterinary surgeon, hung for approximately 2–3 days and then butchered into prime cuts and other products such as sausages and mince.

REGION OF PRODUCTION:

SCOTLAND, HIGHLANDS.

Reestit Mutton

DESCRIPTION:

CURED MUTTON FROM VARIOUS CUTS. COLOUR: PALE CREAM FAT, DEEP
RED LEAN. FLAVOUR: SALTY, MATURE MUTTON. TEXTURE: HARD, DRY.

HISTORY:

Reestit mutton originated in the need to preserve a surplus through
the winter. It was salted and dried by hanging from the rafter (reestit) in
a croft house with an open peat fire; photographs from the early 1900s
show the reestit mutton still hanging from the roof frame though the
fire has been transferred to a range with a chimney. While Shetlanders
continue to reest mutton at home, some Lerwick butchers also cure

the meat. An explanatory notice for visitors in a butcher's window is
headed: 'Reestit Mutton What is it? Traditionally, it was salted lamb
or mutton dried above a peat fire. It will keep for years if you keep it
dry. Reestit mutton soup is an acquired taste that you acquire at the
first taste. A small piece is enough to flavour a pot of soup which
should include cabbage, carrots, neeps and tatties.'

The meat is first used to make stock for broths, then taken out and
eaten separately with potatoes, or chopped finely and returned to the
broth. Alternatively, it can be eaten cold in a Shetland bannock (made
from wheat, not barley or oats), or chopped finely and mixed into
'milgrew', a colloquial term for milk gruel (porridge made with milk).
Reestit mutton is an important feature of the festive food at the Up-
Helly-Aa celebrations in January when platters of the best cuts are
served with bannocks, oatcakes and butter at *ceilidhs* after the ritual
burning of the Viking longboat.

TECHNIQUE:

The meat is cut up and put into a 'secret' brine recipe which one butcher
describes as approximately 80 per cent salt to 20 per cent sugar. It is left
for 10–21 days, then hung on hooks to dry. The recipe in *A Shetland
Cookbook* (1978) requires 'three and a half pounds (1.5kg) of salt; four
quarts (4.5 litres) of water; six ounces (150g) of sugar; two to three
ounces (50–75g) of saltpetre; about sixteen pounds (7.25kg) of mutton'.

Shetland Sassermeat

DESCRIPTION:

A MIXTURE OF RAW, SALTED AND SPICED BEEF, EITHER MOULDED INTO 'SQUARE' SAUSAGES (IN A TIN OF THE TYPE USED FOR LORNE SAUSAGES) WHICH PRODUCES A SLICE APPROXIMATELY 10CM SQUARE AND 1CM THICK, OR SOLD UNSHAPED BY WEIGHT.

HISTORY:

Links with Scandinavia (Shetland was once part of Norway) and the need for a method of preservation that would last through lengthy northern winters have created a number of original Shetland cures for meat and fish. Unlike reestit mutton (which retains its original form), sassermeat, also known as saucermeat, has been modified and is not now intended to last the winter through.

It used to be heavily salted and spiced. Crofters would make a winter's supply all at once, stored in an earthenware crock for use as required. It would be mixed with onions and either fresh meat or bread crumbs, then bound with egg or milk to make fried patties ('bronies') or a baked loaf. Though some traditionalists continue to make their own, most sassermeat is now made by butchers in a milder form.

TECHNIQUE:

Beef and fat are minced together and mixed with rusk, water, salt and a spicing mixture. Each butcher uses a different seasoning and regards his particular formula as a trade secret. Proportions quoted in *A Shetland Cookbook* are 3kg meat and 100g salt mixed with 1 teaspoon each of allspice, black pepper, white pepper, and ground cloves, and half a teaspoon of cinnamon. This can be pressed by hand into a Lorne sausage tin to make a loaf 38cm by 10cm, with sloping sides, weighing about 2kg. The sausage is turned out of this mould and left to set and harden in the refrigerator for several hours before slicing to order.

Shetland Sheep

DESCRIPTION:

SHETLANDS ARE SMALL AND FINE-BONED; THE NATIONAL SHEEP ASSOCIATION COMMENTS THAT THE HILL-BRED WETHER MUTTON 'IS CLAIMED TO BE UNSURPASSABLE'. MEAT IS GENERALLY TENDER, FINE-GRAINED, WELL-FLAVOURED AND SLIGHTLY GAMY, A WELL-FATTENED PRIME LAMB YIELDING A CARCASS OF 11–12KG, ALTHOUGH SOME AS LITTLE AS 8KG. THEY HAVE A LOW PERCENTAGE OF SATURATED FATTY ACIDS.

HISTORY:

Shetlands have long been valued both for meat and for their very fine wool, coloured from white to dark brown. They are the foundation of an important textile industry on the islands. The wool is comparable in fineness to the Merino's and its worth was early recognized by those anxious to encourage domestic resources and manufacture. Shetlands are one of the Scottish primitives. Several are known on the islands, such as the North Ronaldsay (p.76-7). At first, they were spread through the whole of northern Scotland, only dying out on the mainland in the 1880s due to constant cross-breeding, especially with the Cheviot, to develop a more meaty conformation while retaining something of the quality of the wool.

The Shetland Flock Book Society was founded in 1927. After a long period of decline, the primitives are now thought valuable for genetic and commercial reasons. It was never in doubt that it would survive on the islands themselves, but its worth as a grazer of marginal lands has made it among the most popular of British rare breeds. The pure-bred stock remains for breeding but is still much crossed with Cheviots for meat, and has now been awarded Protected Designation of Origin (PDO).

This salt–sugar pickle is the old method for adding character to more mature mutton from native breeds such as the Blackface (Blackie). Reestit Mutton is a variation using native Shetland Sheep which is available from Shetland butchers where the joints are both pickled and then dried. Just as fish smokers in the early nineteenth century modified their smoking cures to produce a more lightly preserved fish, so an early method for mutton is modifed with shorter pickling times.

Catherine Brown

FROM *A YEAR IN A SCOTS KITCHEN*

PICKLE FOR 2-3KG/4LB 8OZ–6LB 12OZ LEG OF MUTTON

2L/3PT 10FLOZ WATER
600G/1LB 5OZ COARSE SEA SALT
250G/9OZ BROWN MUSCOVADO SUGAR
1 SPRIG OF BAY LEAVES
1 SPRIG THYME
5 CRUSHED JUNIPER BERRIES
5 CRUSHED PEPPERCORNS

To pickle:
Put the ingredients into a pan and bring to the boil. Stir to dissolve the salt and sugar and leave to simmer for about ten minutes. Leave to cool.

Put the cold pickle into an earthenware crock or plastic bucket with a lid. Immerse the meat and keep below the surface by laying a heavy plate on top. Cover and keep in a cool place.

Pickle time should be shorter if meat is thin and without bone, longer if it is thick and with bone. For a 3kg/6lb 12oz leg of mutton between twelve and twenty-four hours will produce a well-flavoured result. The longer it is left in the pickle the stronger it becomes.

If kept in a cool dark place, the pickle mixture will keep for several months and can be used again.

To cook the meat:

Rinse under cold water; put into a large pot with three medium onions stuck with three cloves; a sprig of bay leaves; eight peppercorns; three carrots peeled and chopped in two; a small turnip, peeled and chopped roughly in large pieces. Cover with cold water and simmer very gently till the meat is tender. Remove and serve hot with boiled floury potatoes or cold with oatcakes and butter. Use the cooking liquor to make broth. Check first for saltiness and adjust by adding water if necessary. Some of the less choice cuts of meat can be chopped and added to the broth.

Note: This pickle can also be used for pork, duck and chicken.

Shetland sheep are kept on common grazings, where they take care of themselves for much of the year. The breed is hardy and easy to lamb; it is also naturally short-tailed and resistant to foot-rot. Although these breeds are shorn in conventional husbandry systems, they will shed their fleeces naturally in summer if left alone. Excess lambs culled from these flocks in the late summer are used for meat, but some breeding according to the stratified system of production also goes on, in which a first-cross generation is produced using Cheviots. In turn, these are crossed with Suffolks, to give lambs intended solely as meat for the mainland. These crossbred animals are kept on the inbye land. The National Sheep Association remarks, 'It is unlikely that it will ever be supplanted in its native area where the breed will remain as a pure bred stock under the harsher hill conditions, or as a parent stock for the production of cross ewes and lambs under more kindly conditions.'

REGION OF PRODUCTION:
SCOTLAND, SHETLAND ISLANDS.

Smoked Game

HISTORY:
SMOKING WAS A COMMON HIGHLAND METHOD OF PRESERVING SURPLUS GAME FOR USE THROUGHOUT THE WINTER. ORIGINAL METHODS INVOLVED SALTING AND DRYING THE MEAT UNTIL IT WAS QUITE HARD AND THEN HANGING IT FROM RAFTERS ABOVE THE PEAT 'REEK' FROM THE FIRE WHERE IT TOOK ON A STRONG, PEATY FLAVOUR. IT WAS THEN STORED IN COLD, DARK CELLARS, CAVES OR BARNS. AS THE NEED FOR A LESS HIGHLY PRESERVED ITEM DEVELOPED, LIGHTER CURES HAVE BEEN USED AND A SMALL BUT SPECIALIST INDUSTRY IS NOW PRODUCING A CHARACTERFUL PRODUCT WHICH SOME REGARD AS EQUAL TO, IF NOT A BETTER, THAN SMOKED SALMON.

TECHNIQUE:
A venison cure is likely to involve the haunch meat: usually hung for

strain now recognized as Park Soays – they have been used to found flocks on at least 2 other islands. The Hirta Soay strain is derived from animals used to stock the island of Hirta in the St Kilda group when the human population was evacuated in 1930. Some of these sheep were brought to the mainland in 1968 and have been kept separate from other flocks.

TECHNIQUE:

See the remarks about Shetlands, above, for general agricultural matters. Soay are sometimes considered difficult to shepherd, but benefit from frequent handling. Apart from their ornamental value and in situations where high stocking rates are required, Soays are used in reclmation schemes, especially in the South-West of England where wasteland, worked for china clay and then re-seeded, provides a fragile environment on which small, light animals are necessary. Conditions are similar to, if less extreme than, their original home. Meat, from pure-bred animals and from crosses with breeds like Ryelands or Southdowns, is much prized by consumers and is available from specialists.

REGION OF PRODUCTION:

SCOTLAND, ST KILDA GROUP OF ISLANDS.

Aberdeen Rowie

DESCRIPTION:

A MISSHAPEN, UNEVEN, VAGUELY ROUND, FLAKY, FLAT BUN ABOUT 10–20MM DEEP, 80MM DIAMETER AND WEIGHING ABOUT 75G. IT IS SOMETIMES LIKENED TO A CROISSANT WITHOUT THE SHAPE. THERE ARE SEVERAL VARIATIONS ON THE ORIGINAL FORM, FOR EXAMPLE WEE ROWIES (TWO-THIRDS THE NORMAL SIZE), DOUBLE ROWIES (STUCK BACK-TO-BACK WITH BUTTER) AND LOAFIES (MADE WITH ROWIE DOUGH, BUT BAKED IN A BATCH PRODUCING A SQUARE, DEEPER ROWIE). IN SOME PARTS THE DOUGH IS THICKER AND MORE BREAD-LIKE THAN THE ABERDEENSHIRE FLAKY, LAYERED, YEASTED PASTRY. COLOUR: DEEP GOLDEN BROWN FOR WELL-FIRED, 'CREMATED' ROWIES TO PALER GOLDEN

FOR LESS WELL-FIRED 'PALES'. FLAVOUR: A BURNT SALTINESS WHICH IS
LARGELY DETERMINED BY THE DEGREE OF FIRING AND THE FLAVOUR OF
THE FAT.

HISTORY:

These are thought to have developed as a result of the boom in the
fishing industry in Aberdeen around the turn of the last century
when an enterprising baker (origin unknown) was asked to make the
fishermen a roll which would not go stale during their 2–3 week trips
to the fishing grounds. The first literary mention of them is of a
street-seller in Arbroath in 1899: 'Between butteries, Rob Roys [a
kind of Bath bun], and turnovers, her basket was weel filled.'

Although Aberdeen still has more bakers producing their own
distinctive and, they would claim, 'authentic' rowies, others, from
Caithness to Edinburgh, sell what they describe as Aberdeen butteries.
A rowie, or roll, is how they are commonly referred to in Aberdeen.
The term butterie is odd since they are not made with butter. The
name seems to have been given to them by non-Aberdonians, aware
that they are fatty but not realising that the fat used is not butter. Most
bakers use vegetable shortening or lard, though the original
fishermen's rowies were made with butcher's dripping.

TECHNIQUE:

Two doughs are made. One very soft and sticky with very little fat and
the other stiffer with most of the fat. In large bakeries the 2 batches are
mixed by machine for a few seconds only, to preserve the layers. In
smaller bakeries they are folded and rolled by hand in the same way as
puff pastry, using the sticky dough as if it were the butter. Shaping is
invariably by hand. Mechanical devices have been tried: none has been
satisfactory. The dough it is divided into approximately 50g pieces which
are pressed out first with 4 outstretched, floured fingers, then knocked
into their uneven shape with the floured backs of 4 fingers of the left
hand and the floured clenched knuckles of the right. Proved in a warm,
steamy atmosphere for 20 minutes they are baked for 18–20 minutes in
a fairly hot oven. They are left on the tray until stacked on their sides.

Beremeal Bannock

DESCRIPTION:

DISCS 150MM DIAMETER, 12MM THICK. COLOUR: LIGHT GREY-BROWN CRUMB, ROUGH, MEALIE CRUST. FLAVOUR: STRONGER THAN PEARL BARLEY FLOUR, THEY HAVE AN ASTRINGENT, EARTHY TANG, UNSWEETENED.

HISTORY:

Barley was the staple cereal crop in Scotland from Neolithic times until it was progressively displaced by oats (introduced by the Romans) and then by wheat, from the seventeenth century. Barley remained the vital ingredient for beer, whisky distilling, barley broth and barley bannocks; in the Highlands and Islands and among the lower classes in the Lowlands, it continued to be used for making bread. The practice has persisted to this day in the Highland region, particularly in Orkney.

The distinctive form of barley used for bannocks is the variety known as bigg or big (the four-rowed barley, *Hordeum vulgare*). Bigg is called bere or bear (pronounced bare). While the modern bannock is leavened with buttermilk and baking soda, the original was made by cooking the meal first in milk and butter to make a paste. This was then rolled out into thin chapati-like pancakes which were cooked on the girdle or flat iron baking plate. When cooked, they were spread with butter, rolled up tightly and eaten hot. They are still eaten as a savoury part of evening supper in Orkney, accompanied by butter and a slice of fresh, young cheese.

TECHNIQUE:

Modern recipes vary the proportion of beremeal to wheat flour. Most printed Orkney recipes suggest about half and half but some Orcadians make their bannocks with very little wheat flour, preferring the stronger flavour of the beremeal. The flour is mixed with baking soda and buttermilk to make a moist dough which is rolled out and baked on a floured girdle or hot-plate, turning once.

REGION OF PRODUCTION:
NORTH SCOTLAND, ORKNEY.

Scottish Oatcake

DESCRIPTION:

OATCAKES PRODUCED COMMERCIALLY ARE FLAT BISCUITS CONTAINING FLOUR TO BIND THE OATMEAL TO PREVENT BREAKAGE. NON-COMMERCIAL OATCAKES, WITHOUT THE FLOUR AND BAKED IN TRIANGLES ON A GIRDLE, CURL UP AT THE EDGES AS THEY DRY OUT. THE MAIN SHAPES ARE ROUNDS AND FARLS (TRIANGLES) OR CORTERS (QUARTER-CIRCLES OF A LARGE 200MM DISC). OATCAKES ARE 30–100MM DIAMETER, 3–10MM THICK. COLOUR: GREYISH TO LIGHT BROWN. FLAVOUR AND TEXTURE: MEALY, NUTTY.

HISTORY:

These developed in the seventeenth century as oats took over from barley as the staple food grain. The oatcake took its form from the primitive hearthstone cake of meal and water mixed to a paste and spread out to cook on hot stones. At the start, the grains were mixed. 'They make a kind of bread, not unpleasant to the taster of oats and barley, the only grain cultivated in these regions, and from long practice, they have attained considerable skill in moulding the cakes. Of this they eat a little in the morning, and then contentedly go out a hunting, or engage in some other occupation, frequently remaining without any other food till evening' (Buchanan, 1629).

By the early 1800s, however, oatcakes and barley cakes had taken on a separate existence: 'For breakfast the cheese was set out as before, with plenty of butter and barley cakes, and fresh baked oaten cake, which no doubt were made for us; they were kneaded with cream and were excellent' (Dorothy Wordsworth, 1803). Though the habit of mixing with cream is not common today, a recipe, dated

1893, appears in Lady Clark of Tillypronie (1909): '8 oz [250g] of fine oatmeal freshly ground and kept from the air, a pinch of salt, half a teaspoon of baking powder, and as little cream as possible – only just enough to make it into a dough. Too thick cream does not do. Roll it out as thin as possible, and cut it into three-cornered pieces. Put it on the girdle to set. It must not be turned over or it will be tough, but put it on a toaster in front of the fire to brown the top side, toaster sloping towards the fire. To use again it must be re-toasted and sent to table warm. If baked in an oven oatcake will be hard. If without cream, use water with a bit of butter previously melted into it; milk would make flinty cakes. It has no merit if it does not eat short and crisp, but it must not be buttery.'

Despite the attractions of soft white bread, oatcakes have retained their popularity in Scotland where the population continues to consume a higher percentage of hard biscuits than the English. Oatcakes have proved as versatile an accompaniment as bread, since they can be eaten with oily fish like herrings and sardines, cheese of all kinds, jams, jellies, marmalade and honey, or eaten with broth, with a slice of unsalted butter laid – not spread – on top (spread the butter and you break the brittle oatcakes).

TECHNIQUE:

Oatcakes are made with various cuts of ground oatmeal, salt, a little dripping, and water to mix. *Bonnach Imeach* (Hebridean oatcake) is usually made with a fine oatmeal and is rolled out more thickly (5–10mm) than other oatcakes. A thinner, crisper cake (about 3mm thick) is more common. Wheat flour may be added which makes them less brittle. A slightly coarser oatmeal makes them crunchier and rougher.

The dough or paste is rolled out while still hot and cut into shapes which are dried off on a girdle or hot-plate or in the oven. Only hand-made oatcakes made on a girdle will curl at the edges.

REGION OF PRODUCTION:

NORTH SCOTLAND AND GENERAL SCOTLAND.

Water Biscuit

DESCRIPTION:

A THICK CIRCULAR BISCUIT ABOUT 85–90MM DIAMETER, 5–8MM THICK.
WEIGHT: ABOUT 20G. COLOUR: IRREGULAR CREAM TO PALE GOLD,
BLISTERED IN PLACES WITH GOLD-BROWN BUBBLES, DOCKED WITH
SMALL HOLES. FLAVOUR AND TEXTURE: RICH, NUTTY FLAVOUR,
EXTREMELY CRISP, WITH FLAKY TEXTURE.

HISTORY:

Water biscuits are the principal survivors of a class developed from ship's biscuits, formerly of great importance in the British Isles. These hard biscuits which, as the name suggests, originated as bread substitutes for provisioning ships, developed into more palatable forms in the late 1800s, evolving, with a little enrichment, through 'Captain's Biscuits' into water biscuits. The latter were well known when a recipe given by Harris and Borella (*c.* 1900) instructs soft flour, a little salt and sufficient water to make a tight dough; this was then folded and worked intensively through the rollers of a biscuit-brake. The recipes developed further with small enrichments of fat and sugar.

Although a number of companies still make water biscuits in different parts of the UK, there is good evidence for various regional types in Scotland. *Law's Grocer's Manual*, roughly contemporary with the recipe above, remarks on the use of different flours by manufacturers, the English typically using moderately soft flour (giving a hard, crisp biscuit which offered some resistance to the teeth), and strong flour being favoured in western Scotland, resulting in a more coloured, flaky appearance and biscuits which were more easily broken. Gardens and Stockans Water Biscuits and Black's Water Biscuits, both trademarks, are examples of this type. They contrast strongly both in thickness and texture with Carr's Table Water Biscuits and Jacob's Cream Crackers, the varieties made and best known in England.

REGION OF PRODUCTION:

SCOTLAND, ORKNEY ISLANDS.

Heather Ale

DESCRIPTION:

HEATHER ALE IS AMBER-GOLD AND HAS A FLOWERY, AROMATIC FLAVOUR, WITH A BITTER NOTE. IT IS 4 PER CENT ALCOHOL BY VOLUME (CASK ALE), 5 PER CENT ALCOHOL BY VOLUME (BOTTLED VERSION). PICTISH ALE IS 5.4 PER CENT ALCOHOL BY VOLUME.

HISTORY:

Neolithic remains from the Inner Hebrides include pottery with residues indicating it had held a fermented beverage containing heather. There are many references from the Middle Ages onwards to beers brewed with heather and other herbs, especially bog myrtle. Such drinks survived the introduction of brewing methods from continental Europe in some areas of the west and north of Scotland, especially Galloway and the remoter parts of the Highlands and Islands. The traveller Pennant encountered heather ale in Islay in the eighteenth century, and McNeill, writing in 1956, recalls a woman on Orkney who made it. The Islands were remote from mainstream brewing practices, with no major commercial brewers until the twentieth century; consequently, the habit of brewing with local herbs, rather than hops, survived and remains as a tradition of home-brewing. Recently, heather ale has been revived as a commercial product by a Glasgow company, Heather Ale Ltd, who began to develop a recipe translated from Gaelic in the mid-1980s. It is marketed as 'Fraoch' (pronounced fruich); *leann fraoch* is Gaelic for heather ale.

TECHNIQUE:

Heather for this beer is gathered from bell heather (*Erica cinerea*) and ling (*Calluna vulgaris*), 2 species native to the British Isles. It is cut during the flowering season, in shoots 8–10cm long, including the young leaves and flowers. To make the beer, Scotch ale malt is sparged (sprayed with hot water) to extract the malt sugars, giving a solution called wort. The wort is boiled in a brew kettle, to which heather and a small quantity of hops are added; after boiling, the mixture is run through a hop-back (sieve) in which fresh heather is placed. Brewer's yeast is added, and the wort allowed to ferment for several days, depending on the alcoholic strength desired; more heather flowers are laid on the top during this time. The beer is conditioned in bulk for about 10 days until the appropriate carbon dioxide level is reached; during this process it is fined and then filtered into casks or bottles as appropriate. The bottles are capped and pasteurized, the casks stoppered and distributed with no further treatment. Heather ale is produced in early June–early December; the cask-conditioned ale is available July–October; the bottled ale from July until early spring; the stronger Pictish Ale is made as a Christmas or New Year drink.

REGION OF PRODUCTION:
WEST SCOTLAND AND GENERAL SCOTLAND.

Silver Birch Wine

DESCRIPTION:
THE WINE IS A PALE STRAW COLOUR, WITH A LIGHT, DRY, CLEAN, REFRESHING FLAVOUR.

HISTORY:
Records of the use of birch sap to make alcoholic drinks go back at least 200 years in Scotland. 'Quantities of excellent wine,' says Thomas Pennant, writing of the Highlands (1796), 'are extracted from the live tree (silver birch) by tapping.' Mrs Dalgairns (1829) instructed, 'Bore a hole in a tree and put in a faucet, and it will run for 2 or 3 days together without hurting the tree; then put in a pin to stop it, and next year you may draw as much from the same hole.' The same drink was called 'Birk' wine by Meg Dods in 1826; her recipe was, 'To every gallon of the sap of the birch tree, boiled, put four pounds of white sugar, and the thin paring of a lemon. Boil and skim this well. When cool, put fresh yeast to it. Let it ferment for four or five days; then close it up. Keep the bung very close, and in four months rack it off and bottle it.'

This wine is noted by Queen Victoria in her journals as being one of Prince Albert's favourite drinks. It is also mentioned in the annals of

Moniack Castle and it was the evidence of this tradition which encouraged the present owner Phillipa Fraser to start making Silver Birch wine commercially at her ancestral home in 1982. The wine-making business has developed well and they now also make elderflower, meadowsweet, raspberry and bramble wines as well as sloe gin and mead.

The wine was also known in other parts of Britain, *vide* the recipes in John Evelyn's MS cookery book (*c.* 1700), Richard Bradley (1736), Hannah Glasse (1747) and Mrs Raffald (1769) – who also suggests sycamore wine by the same process. A 'traditional birch wine' is made today in Cawston, Norfolk using birch sap and grape juice. It should be noted in this context that the word 'wine' has been used colloquially in English for centuries to denote drinks of 8–14 per cent alcohol fermented from fruit, flowers and vegetables.

TECHNIQUE:

Sap for birch wine made in Scotland is collected from trees in the area around the winery. In the spring when the sap is rising, holes are bored 1m up the tree and 2.5cm into the wood, a cork is put in and attached to a plastic tube running into a 5-gallon drum, which fills up with sap. Once the sap has been collected, the hole is stopped. The sap is mixed with yeast, sugar and water, and allowed to ferment. It matures for 9 months before bottling.

REGION OF PRODUCTION:

NORTH SCOTLAND, EAST ANGLIA.

Beremeal

DESCRIPTION:

COLOUR: GREY-BROWN. FLAVOUR: STRONGER THAN PEARL BARLEY FLOUR, AN ASTRINGENT EARTHY TANG.

HISTORY:

Despite the fact that today barley is mainly malted and used for whisky, it was the main cereal crop in Scotland from Neolithic times until the introduction of oats. Oats were used increasingly as the grain staple for human consumption, although they only consolidated their position after the seventeenth century. For most Scots, barley then became the grain for beer and whisky and was marginalized as a foodstuff. But barley breads continued to be eaten by poorer people in the Lowlands until improvements in agricultural practice and import of foreign grain brought wheaten bread to a wider public. This change did not, however, reach as far as the Scottish Highlands and Islands, where barley continued to be an important staple used for bread in the form of a flat, girdle-baked bannock. Most of the bere grown today comes from Orkney and it is the Orcadians who preserve the tradition of making the beremeal bannock. The distinctive form of barley used is the Northern variety known as bigg or big (the four-rowed barley, *Hordeum vulgare*). Bigg is called bere or bear (pronounced bare). Most of the beremeal comes from a mill on Orkney and another at Golspie (Sutherland).

TECHNIQUE:
Beremeal is kiln-dried and stone-ground into fine flour.

REGION OF PRODUCTION:
NORTH SCOTLAND.

Rowan Jelly

DESCRIPTION:
THIS IS CRIMSON RED WITH A SWEET-ASTRINGENT FLAVOUR. OTHER FRUIT PRODUCE DIFFERENT COLOURS: SLOE, DARK PURPLE; HAWTHORN, PALE RUBY RED; WILD CHERRY, DARK RUBY RED; BRAMBLE, BLACKISH-PURPLE.

HISTORY:
The jelly from wild Highland berries was originally used as a reviving drink – a spoonful mixed with boiling water, whisky or rum – or as a sweet pudding with cream. The drink is mentioned by St Fond (1784) in his account of travels in the Hebrides. A description of jellies with cream as a dessert appears in an account by young Elizabeth Grant of Rothimurchus when visiting a relative in 1812. Inside her hostess's

deep-shelved pantry, beside the butter, honey, sweetmeats and spiced whisky, were pots of preserved jellies. The cook skimmed some cream off the milk, emptied the whole pot of jelly on a plate and poured over the cream. The dish, she explains, was known as 'bainne briste' meaning broken milk.

Several companies make rowan jelly but the pioneer of preserves from wild fruits has been Phillipa Fraser, of Moniack Wineries, who started collecting berries as a consequence of country wine-making.

TECHNIQUE:
The berries are gathered, beginning in late summer with wild cherries and running through to late autumn for rowan and sloes. After cleaning, they are boiled with apples (which contribute pectin) in water to produce a juice; this is strained and boiled with sugar until setting point is reached. Commonly there are 60g berries per 100g of jelly. Total sugar content is 60g per 100g.

REGION OF PRODUCTION:
NORTH SCOTLAND.

Peasemeal

DESCRIPTION:
ROASTED, MILLED PEAS, A BROWN-YELLOW POWDER WHOSE TEXTURE VARIES A LITTLE ACCORDING TO HUMIDITY, FROM FINE AND SMOOTH TO VERY SLIGHTLY GRITTY; THE FLAVOUR IS QUITE STRONG AND EARTHY.

HISTORY:
Flour ground from peas and foods made from it, notably brose (a soup or porridge) and bannocks, have a long history in Scotland, especially as food for the common people. McNeill (1929) mentions pease bannocks, instructing that they were made in the same manner as barley bannocks – that is, the flour was mixed with water, milk or whey, rolled thinly and baked on a girdle. She quotes a much earlier reference to pease scones (a similar type of bread) from the early eighteenth century. Macleod, in her foreword to McLintock (1736),

remarks that pease and bean meal were baked into bread and that pease meal has survived in the Orkneys and North-East Scotland. In the twentieth century it was a food associated with poverty and is now mostly consumed by the elderly.

Peasemeal is considered very digestible. For brose it is mixed with boiling liquid, usually water, and consumed straight away. This is a form of convenience food, made quickly, and eaten with butter and pepper or salt, or with sugar and raisins. Uses in the modern kitchen include adding it to soups and stews and as a vegetarian food, especially for pastes flavoured with herbs and garlic.

TECHNIQUE:

Yellow field peas imported from eastern England are used for this product. They are roasted gently, a process which caramelizes some of the sugar, makes more starch and protein available for digestion and darkens the colour. They are ground through 3 pairs of water-powered millstones, becoming successively finer with each set. There is one miller of peasemeal at Golspie (Sutherland).

REGION OF PRODUCTION:

NORTH EAST SCOTLAND.

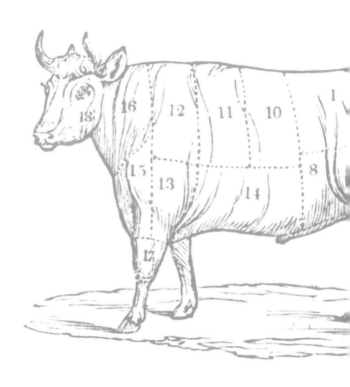

***

Also produced in North Scotland
CROWDIE CHEESE (P.106-7)
DUNLOP CHEESE (P.11-13)
FINNIAN HADDOCK (P20-1)
KALE (P.1)

Scotland: Countrywide

'Floury' Potatoes

ROUND OR OVAL-SHAPED, FIRM TUBERS OF VARYING SIZES AND WEIGHTS. THE 2 MOST COMMON VARIETIES ARE: GOLDEN WONDER, WITH A RUSSET SKIN AND WHITE FLESH, A STRONG FLAVOUR AND ELONGATED PEAR-SHAPE; KERR'S PINK, WHICH HAS A PARTLY PINK SKIN, CREAM FLESH, A DISTINCTIVE FLAVOUR, AND IS A ROUND SHAPE.

HISTORY:

By the nineteenth century, farm carts selling 'mealy tatties' (dry floury potatoes boiled in salted water) had become a common sight on the streets of Scottish cities. This type of potato, favoured by the Scots, has a dry, powdery surface when cooked, and a stronger, more dominant flavour than most available in the British market. Potatoes had been gradually accepted in Scotland during the late eighteenth and early nineteenth centuries, especially in areas of impoverished peasantry. The crop became very important in the West and the Islands. *An Account of the Economic History of the Hebrides and Highlands* (1808) states that by about 1763 the people were subsisting on potatoes for 9 months of the year. Potatoes also combined well with the northern Scots' staple diet of milk and fish. 'Fish with oat bread or potatoes, without any accompaniment at all, forms the three daily meals of the Shetland cottager,' said E. Edmondston, in *Sketches and Tales of the Shetland Isles* (1856). Annette Hope (1987) cites numerous references to illustrate the importance of potatoes to the inhabitants of western and northern Scotland. Both she and Jeremy Cherfas (1995) comment on regional preferences for floury varieties which exist in western Scotland down to the present day.

Many floury varieties have been raised, including Dunbar Rover, Arran Victory, Duke of York and Champion as well as Golden Wonder and Kerr's Pink. Golden Wonder was raised in 1906 by John Brown near Arbroath; it remains one of the varieties with the highest amount of dry matter. Kerr's Pink was raised by James Henry in 1907 and was originally known as Henry's Seedling until it won the Lord Derby Gold Medal at the Ormskirk Trials in 1916. Its merits were recognized by a seedsman (Mr Kerr) who bought the seed and renamed it in 1917.

TECHNIQUE:

Growing underground, potatoes have an advantage over grain crops in a climate which tends towards high rainfall and strong winds; and the rain and cool temperatures also suit the crop. Potatoes flourish in the poor soils of the Scottish Highlands, although for commercial growth, areas of flatter land are favoured – in Ayrshire, on the West coast, and in the fertile soils of East and Central Scotland from Aberdeenshire to the Borders. In the nineteenth century, potatoes were cultivated on a system of hand-dug furrows known as 'lazy beds', whose remains can be seen in many remote parts of the West Highlands. Cultivation is now mechanized. The Scots have particular expertise in the development of new potato varieties, originally derived from the realisation that potato blight would otherwise seriously affect the crop.

March is the main month for early potato planting, April for maincrop. Disease-free seed potatoes are planted in drills in clod-free soils. Harvesting starts in September and is mostly mechanized. All potatoes are lifted by the end of October. They may be sold immediately or treated with sprout-suppressants and fungicides and stored in cool conditions excluding light. Though neither Golden Wonder nor Kerr's Pink are grown on a large scale, the demand remains. Recently, increased interest in potato varieties has led to more attention to their qualities.

REGION OF PRODUCTION:

SCOTLAND.

Tayberry, Tummelberry

DESCRIPTION:

TAYBERRY: A LONG FRUIT (ABOUT 4CM), DEEP PURPLE-RED WHEN FULLY RIPE, WITH A SWEET AND AROMATIC FLAVOUR. TUMMELBERRY: DEEPER RED WITH A SLIGHTLY ROUNDER FRUIT AND SHARPER, LESS AROMATIC FLAVOUR.

HISTORY:

Tayberries and Tummelberries (named for rivers whose valleys disgorge on the Strathmore area, the main berry-producing region of eastern Scotland) are derived from a long tradition of fruit cross-breeding which began in America in the 1860s with Judge Logan's berry when he set about crossing a cultivated (and too bland for his liking) blackberry with a wild variety with more flavour.

The Tayberry is a hybrid of an unnamed raspberry bred at the Scottish Crop Research Institute at Invergowrie (1978) and the blackberry cultivar Aurora from Oregon. The Tummelberry is a newer hybrid, obtained by crossing the Tayberry with one of its sister hybrids (1984). The Scottish contribution, particularly the Tayberry, is now grown widely in the USA as a commercial crop with a plant patent, also in France, Germany, Holland and Scandinavia, while at home it has established itself most successfully on farms which have a pick-your-own facility.

TECHNIQUE:

Tayberries and Tummelberries are commercially cultivated in the open, on a post and wire support system. Like blackberries, they grow best in well-drained, medium loam with a pH of about 6.5 and do best on sites with a sheltered, sunny aspect.

REGION OF PRODUCTION:

SOUTH SCOTLAND AND GENERAL SCOTLAND.

Crowdie Cheese

DESCRIPTION:

PASTEURIZED, SOFT COW'S MILK CHEESE. THERE ARE SOME VARIANTS. GRUTH DHU (BLACK CROWDIE): CROWDIE MIXED WITH DOUBLE CREAM AND ROLLED IN TOASTED OATMEAL AND BLACK PEPPER. HRAMSA: CROWDIE MIXED WITH WILD GARLIC AND WHITE AND RED PEPPER. GALIC HRAMSA: ROLLED IN CRUMBLED FLAKED HAZELNUTS AND ALMONDS. CROWDIE IS SOLD IN PLASTIC TUBS OF APPROXIMATELY 150G; GRUTH DHU IN CYLINDRICAL ROLLS OF APPROXIMATELY 125G, UP TO 1KG; HRAMSA AND GALIC IN ROLLS OF 125G; HIGHLAND SOFT IN TUBS OF 150G. COLOUR: CREAM OR WHITE. FLAVOUR: SHARP, ACIDIC, REFRESHING.

HISTORY:

Crowdie was at one time the universal breakfast dish of Scotland. In the seventeenth century the name was applied to foods akin to porridge – mixtures of oatmeal and water which had a slightly curdled texture (*OED*). There were various developments of this in the Lowlands but in the Highlands, by the nineteenth century, the word had come to denote a species of milk curd.

Today, the Lowland meaning has been replaced entirely and crowdie has become known solely as the Highlanders' soft cheese. It is of ancient origin, probably having roots in Pictish or Viking practices, and linked to a system of transhumance, in which cattle, sheep and goats were taken to mountain pastures and the milk made into butter and cheese. Surplus crowdie was mixed with butter, packed in earthenware crocks, then covered with a sealing layer of melted butter. These were kept in a cool barn for use through the winter. This was known as crowdie-butter.

This butter and the way of life that engendered it were stopped by the Highland Clearances. The commercial revival of the soft crowdie is almost entirely due to the pioneering efforts of Susanna Stone and her late husband Reggie, who started making it for sale in the early 1960s. They were post-war revivalist farmhouse cheese-makers who in the early days battled against bureaucracy to produce the native cheese. 'The great treat,' said G.W. Lockhart in *The Scot and his Oats* (1983), 'was to have crowdie mixed with fresh cream and piled on an oatcake with fresh salted butter. Then you had a royal feast of flavours – acid, sweet and salt, and better perhaps, a royal mixture of textures, soft, crisp and crunchy.'

TECHNIQUE:
The traditional croft method, described by Susanna Stone as made by her mother, was to leave the bowl of milk at the fireside in winter or in a warm place in summer. It soured natur- ally and formed a curd. The curds were cooked lightly, until they scrambled (the curd and whey separated). The curds were poured into a muslin-lined bowl and the ends of the muslin were drawn together and tied with string. The bag was hung from a branch of a tree for a few days to drip, or over the tap in the sink, until most of the whey drained out.

The modern method, made by Susanna Stone, follows the old by souring the milk with a starter and allowing it to curd without rennet. The scrambling procedure is followed and the curd is hung in muslin bags to drain. Others now make crowdie, though not all in the old way without rennet. Flavourings are added by some brands to suit the modern palate.

REGION OF PRODUCTION:
NORTH SCOTLAND AND GENERAL SCOTLAND.

Scottish Cheddar Cheese

DESCRIPTION:
MOSTLY PASTEURIZED, HARD, COW'S MILK CHEESE; A FEW SMALL FARMHOUSE CHEDDARS FROM UNPASTEURIZED MILK. COLOUR: PALE YELLOW, OR ARTIFICIALLY COLOURED ORANGE-YELLOW. FORM: ROUNDS, PLASTIC-WRAPPED, WAX-DIPPED AND CLOTHBOUND; ALSO RINDLESS BLOCKS. FLAVOUR: 12–14-MONTH-OLD WILL HAVE A SHARP BITE TO IT, WHILE A 4–5-MONTH-OLD WILL BE MORE MELLOW AND ROUNDED. MATURITY CLASSIFICATION: MILD; MEDIUM MATURE; MATURE; EXTRA MATURE; VINTAGE.

The rise of Scottish Cheddar occurred with the growth of the cities of central Scotland, particularly Glasgow and Paisley, in the late nineteenth century. It developed from the Ayrshire Dunlop, which was significantly improved after the Ayrshire Agricultural Association brought a Somerset farmer and his wife to teach the Cheddar method in 1885.

The subsequent decline – though not extinction – of Dunlop came about during World War II. Milk was bought in bulk by Milk Marketing Boards and trucked to large creameries to make a cheese by the cheddaring method which they subsequently described as Cheddar. Though it might just as easily have retained the name of the old Ayrshire cheese, the MMBs believed at that time that Dunlop presented the wrong marketing image, having the same name as a leading tyre company of the day. Only in some creameries, notably on Arran and Islay, was the name preserved. Elsewhere, Scottish cheddared cheese of Dunlop ancestry took the Cheddar tag. There are now several variants, such as Orkney, Arran, Rothsay, Islay, Campbeltown, Galloway, Lockerbie.

TECHNIQUE:

Made from pasteurized cow's milk following the basic Cheddar method.

REGION OF PRODUCTION:

SCOTLAND.

Crab (Scotland)

DESCRIPTION:

WIDTH ACROSS THE SHELL UP TO 300MM; MINIMUM LEGAL SIZE 125MM. COLOUR: REDDISH, PINK-BROWN TINTED WITH PURPLE, LEGS REDDISH AND CLAWS BLACK. FLAVOUR: STRONG DARK (LIVER) MEAT, WHITE MEAT IS MORE DELICATE THAN LOBSTER.

HISTORY:

There is archaeological evidence for the use of shellfish of all types in the West of Scotland from at least 5,000 BC. It appears likely that the crab was a common item of food for coastal communities eking out a living from a meagre environment. Crabs were more easily caught than lobsters and became more integrated into the daily diet, providing a useful supply of high-quality protein. In Scotland the brown crab was known in the dialect as a partan; under this name they were cried through the streets of Georgian Edinburgh, and 'partan's taes', or toes, i.e. crab claws, were counted amongst the delicacies served in taverns.

The extensive East-coast fishery for crabs must have developed after the building of railheads at the ports during the nineteenth century. This allowed it to tap an expanding market among the middle classes in large towns of Scotland and England (Hope, 1987).

As if to celebrate their place in the national diet, Scottish recipes for crab abound. For instance, they flavoured soups, the most famous being the creamy broth Partan Bree; a Victorian recipe for this was recorded by Lady Clark of Tillypronie (1909).

Although many other British districts have a long connection with crab fishing, for instance Cromer, or Dartmouth and Kingswear in Devon, it is argued that the crab landed from Scottish waters has a finer and more intense flavour from rich feeding in unpolluted, cold northern waters.

TECHNIQUE:

Caught in deep-water lobster pots (creels) with fresh fish bait. May be sold live, frozen or processed. At centres of intensive crab fishing, plants have been set up to boil the crabs in large tanks and to remove the meat (mostly by hand) before packing and freezing.

REGION OF PRODUCTION:

SCOTLAND.

Lobster (Scotland)

DESCRIPTION:

CARAPACE LENGTH UP TO 45CM; IT IS ILLEGAL TO LAND LOBSTERS WITH A CARAPACE SHELL OF UNDER 85MM.

HISTORY:

As part of the general foraging for seafood, to eke out a meagre diet from the produce of the land, the European lobster, *Homarus gammarus*, was eaten by those living in coastal areas of Scotland. By the nineteenth century, however, there is evidence that it had been taken up by Scottish gourmets, notably in the gathering of gastronomes known as the Cleikum Club where their recipe for 'Lobster Haut Gout' tells the cook: 'Pick the firm meat from a parboiled lobster or two and take also the inside, if not thin and watery. Season highly with white pepper, cayenne, pounded mace, and cloves, nutmeg and salt. Take a little well-flavoured gravy – for example the jelly of roast veal – a few tiny bits of butter, a spoonful of soy or walnut catsup, or of any favourite flavoured vinegar, and a spoonful of red wine. Stew the cut lobster in this sauce for a few minutes.'

The association of Scotland with lobster, over and above any other shellfishery in Britain, has much to do with its plentiful supply and the distinctive and intense flavour produced by rich feeding in clear, cold, unpolluted waters. After commercial creel fishing began in the mid-eighteenth century, catches of live lobsters in Orkney were put into floating chests or 'keep boxes' and collected each week by large fishing boats which took them to the London market. In the 1970s around 60 boats were creel fishing for lobsters in the Orkneys.

TECHNIQUE:

Caught live in baited lobster pots (creels) in rocky areas.

REGION OF PRODUCTION:

SCOTLAND.

The clootie dumpling has been made in the glen for generations, and is still commonly produced in Scotland to this day. It is a wonderful winter pudding, though it can also be served for afternoon tea and is often eaten sliced and fried for breakfast.

The clootie dumpling is made of flour, baking soda, currants, raisins, suet, ginger, cinnamon, syrup and treacle, brown sugar, bread crumbs, grated carrot, milk and – traditionally – a silver sixpence. The word 'clootie' comes from the cloth (or 'clootie') bag in which flour was bought and in which the dumpling is cooked.

To cook the dumpling, put the cloth bag into boiling water for five minutes, then take it out and wring it dry with a wooden spurtle or spoon (though be warned, there's a knack involved). Dust the outside of the bag with flour to stop the water penetrating it, then pour the combined ingredients into the bag and draw it up tightly with a string. The end result should resemble a cannonball. Boil the bag for two to three hours, and serve the dumpling hot with cream. *(See recipe for Clootie Dumpling, p. 379)*

Tom Lewis

CHEF, MONACHYLE MHOR, HIGHLAND PERTHSHIRE

Salmon (Scotland)

DESCRIPTION:

ADULT SALMON ARE LIKELY TO BE 80CM–1M LONG. WEIGHT: 4–30KG.
COLOUR: SILVER ALONG BELLY TURNING TO BLUE-BLACK ALONG BACK,
INTERNAL COLOUR VARYING SHADES OF REDDISH-PINK ACCORDING TO
FEEDING AND CONDITION.

HISTORY:

Early salmon fisheries on the rivers Tay, Spey, Tweed, Don and Dee produced large catches which were eaten fresh in summer and kippered (smoked and dried) in winter. The quantity caught each year was such that it was one of the most common foods of the people and became so firmly fixed in the minds of the upper classes in Scotland as a cheap, working-man's food that a Highland gentleman, on visiting London, made the mistake of choosing beef for himself and salmon for his servant: 'The Cook, who attended him humoured the Jest, and the Master's eating was Eight Pence and Duncan's came to almost as many Shillings' (Burt, *Letters from the North of Scotland,* 1730).

While supplies of wild salmon remained plentiful for the best part of the last century, there has since been a gradual decline. Over-fishing and netting have been just two of the problems; research is being undertaken to discover the reasons.

Salmon have, of course, been caught in many other rivers as long as they have been prey to Scottish fishermen. There is no simple difference between a Scottish and an English salmon. However, the number and wealth of Scottish streams and their lack of pollution has meant that Scottish Salmon is a regional descriptor of some force and meaning. It has become more distinct and valid with the growth of salmon farming in the last 30 years. As demand for fresh fish increased around the world – and the means to deliver matched the possibilities of sale – so stocks in the wild came under pressure. The expansion of salmon farming, almost exclusively in Scottish waters, was therefore timely. Common standards among producers will allow the existence of rigid quality markers. This is regional food in the making.

Farming began on the West Coast in 1969 and has spread to the Islands, above all the Shetlands, where they market their salmon separately from the rest of Scotland. There have been problems with farmed salmon, but aquaculture has brought employment to a remote and declining population whose traditions have always been based on harvesting from the sea. Many problems have been solved and much research undertaken to farm more efficiently and with less damage to the environment. Skilled farming can produce a high-quality fish which has made its name in the markets of Europe, gaining a French Label Rouge accolade of prime quality.

TECHNIQUE:

During their lifespan salmon go through various stages: in the wild, very young fish, or fry, are at risk from predators and starvation. But after about 3 months in river water, if they survive, they change into parr and then, 1–4 years later, when they are large and strong enough, they change into smolts. They have silvery skins and are, in effect, miniature salmon. Smolts go to sea and feed extensively. Their feeding grounds are thought to be off Greenland and the Faroe Islands. Migration from river and sea generally takes place in early summer, which is another time of high mortality for wild fish.

After only a year at sea, some of the smolts return to the river to spawn; they weigh about 2.25kg, and are known as grilse. The remaining fish stay at sea, growing by about 2.25kg a year. When they return as salmon to fresh water to spawn, it is to their home river where they were hatched. The best quality are caught early in the season when still fat and flavoursome from the rich sea feeding grounds. They are likely to weigh from 8lb to about 60lb. When, and if, they reach their place of hatching and the female spawns and the male ejects his milt on top of the spawn, they become either spent kelts and die from exhaustion and lack of food, or mended kelts and make it back to the sea. Around 5 per cent return to spawn again. They will usually spend 2–3 winters in the sea, sometimes up to 5. The oldest recorded salmon, caught on Loch Maree in Wester Ross, was 13 years old and had spawned 4 times.

Salmon farming depends on breeding stocks which are milked for their eggs in November. The eggs are checked to ensure they are free from disease and they are kept in controlled conditions until they hatch in March. The young fish are very tiny and are carefully monitored. They are reared in special tanks, and as they grow in size are transferred to larger tanks in freshwater lochs, where they grow until they are large enough to be transferred to the sea farms in lochs fed by sea water.

The main practical difference between farmed and wild salmon is that the first is available all year. The debate about the difference in eating quality will long continue. The best farmed fish approach the wild in texture and taste.

REGION OF PRODUCTION:
SCOTLAND.

Smoked Eel

DESCRIPTION:
EELS FOR SMOKING ARE 45–50CM LONG. WEIGHT: MAXIMUM 4KG, BUT EELS FOR SMOKING ARE USUALLY AROUND 500G. THEY MAY BE SOLD WHOLE, UNFILLETED OR FILLETED, IN VACUUM PACKS FROM 115G UPWARDS. COLOUR: ADULT FISH ARE USUALLY BLACK, GREEN-BLACK OR GREY-BROWN ON BACK AND SIDES AND YELLOWISH BELOW; INTERNAL FLESH, DARK CREAM. FLAVOUR: WOODY-OILY, SUCCULENT, SALTY.

HISTORY:
Recently, a number of small Scottish smokers have made use of the abundant supplies of common eels (*Anguilla anguilla*) in some rivers, most notably the Tweed. The Tweed Salmon Fishers Association has given exclusive eel-catching rights to a local smoker who has been trusted not to catch salmon.

There is also a certain amount of farming of eels, one farm claims production of 100,000 eels per annum.

TECHNIQUE:

The eel-catcher/smoker takes his supply of eels in the autumn as they return to the sea after feeding. A fyke net is used for catching them; this is strung across the river, deflecting the eels left or right into closed ends where they are trapped. The fish are first starved in the river for about 2 weeks. After killing, they are immersed in brine then cold-smoked over oak chips for 6–7 hours. They are finished over hot smoke, which cooks them through, for about 3 hours.

REGION OF PRODUCTION:
SCOTLAND.

Smoked Salmon (Scotland)

DESCRIPTION:
SOLD IN WHOLE, TRIMMED SIDES WEIGHING 675G–2KG, OR IN SMALLER PACKS. COLOUR AND FLAVOUR VARY ACCORDING TO THE CURE AND THE QUALITY OF THE FISH – FROM THE INTENSE PEATINESS OF A WILD FISH WHICH HAS BEEN SLOWLY SMOKED OVER PEAT, TO VERY LIGHTLY SALTED AND DELICATELY SMOKED FARMED SALMON. 'ALL SMOKED SALMON IS NOT CREATED EQUAL. MOST AFICIONADOS GIVE THE NOD TO SMOKED SCOTCH SALMON AS THE BEST. IT IS, AS A RULE, THE LEAST OILY, THE MOST SUBTLY FLAVOURED, HAS THE FIRMEST AND MOST PLEASING TEXTURE AND THE LEAST AMOUNT OF SALT.'

HISTORY:
Preservation of salmon began with a method known as kippering, recorded early, in a document dated 1479, when a fishery was obliged to deliver 3 dozen salmon a year, either 'fresh or kippered', to a monastery in Fife.

The salmon sent for kippering had spawned and were therefore no longer in their prime. They were 'spent', lacking fat and moisture, hence easier to pickle and smoke. The Dutch word *kuppen*, meaning to spawn, was applied originally to a spent fish. By association, it was also applied to a kippered or spent salmon which had been cured. Kippered salmon is mentioned in the household book of King James V (d. 1542).

From an expedient way to deal with less-than-prime fish, a smoked salmon industry has developed with a variety of cures, for both wild and farmed fish, to suit all tastes, but with a jealously guarded reputation of quality. To safeguard this, a quality approval specification has now been drawn up covering all aspects of production. There is a Certified Quality Mark governing smoked salmon.

TECHNIQUE:

There was a time when kippering salmon was a job for the domestic cook – like the Scandinavians who continue to cure gravlax at home. McNeill (1929) describes 'To Kipper Salmon: A Modern Method', involving salt, demerara sugar, olive oil, rum or whisky. She suggests that the best flavour will be achieved if the fish is smoked in an outside shed without windows, used as a kiln, over a mixture of peat, oak chips and juniper wood.

Today, cures are all commercial and recipes closely guarded secrets. The basic method involves filleted sides. Salting may be dry or wet, the intention is to stabilize salt content to a minimum of approximately 3.5 per cent. The most common method is to lay the fish on trays of salt and sprinkle more salt over them by hand, how much extra depends on the taste of the customer. They are left for 12–24 hours. Smokehouses may add their own ingredients – sugar, juniper berries, herbs, molasses, rum or whisky – at the salting stage. Fillets are washed and left overnight to dry, laid out on wire mesh trays then wheeled on trolleys into electronically controlled smoking kilns. They are cold-smoked at 20–30°C, usually over smouldering oak chips, though some smokers continue to use peat. During the process, the temperature and moisture content are monitored and controlled. Some curers rest, or mature, the fish for 3–4 days at a low temperature.

REGION OF PRODUCTION:
SCOTLAND.

Beef Shorthorn

DESCRIPTION:

AVERAGE LIVE-WEIGHT OF BULL AGED 16 MONTHS, 622KG. FLESH DEEPLY RED, WELL- MARBLED WITH INTRA-MUSCULAR CREAM FAT. FLAVOUR AT ITS BEST WHEN IT HAS BEEN HUNG 2–3 WEEKS.

HISTORY:

The Beef Shorthorn, or 'The Great Improver' as it has often been called, has a recorded history of over 200 years and has played a major part in the beef industry throughout the world. It is generally thought the pure Shorthorn was developed in Yorkshire in the late eighteenth century. The distinct yet related Scotch Shorthorn (later described as the Beef Shorthorn) was the consequence of work begun in the 1830s when Amos Cruickshank of Sittyton and his brother became tenants of an Aberdeenshire farm. By the 1870s, Cruickshank's bull calves were being sold to his neighbours for breeding. New herds were being built up and it was from this source of beef cattle that the breed was born. The beefy type of Shorthorn was eventually treated as a separate breed from the Dairy Shorthorn.

By the 1940s and 1950s, Beef Shorthorns were numbered in thousands and emphasis was put on the export market. The fashion was for early maturing 'baby beef', short and dumpy by today's standards. Fat animals were the order of the day and in the following decades the breed suffered a decline. As a result of some dedicated supporters, however, who have modernized the breed to ensure it meets the requirements of height and smooth fleshing, while still retaining the other qualities of flavour and character in the meat, it has experienced substantial revival. Because modern beef consumption requires a higher quality and taste, there has been a return to native breeds such as the Shorthorn. The bulk of the national herd is in Scotland, the remainder principally in North Yorkshire.

TECHNIQUE:

Beef Shorthorn are used in regions where there is a need for extensive farming, where ease of calving and hardiness are essential. Their eyes, skin pigment and coat texture ensure a greater tolerance of extreme weather conditions and their excellent feet and legs make them ideal for ranching. Carcasses are hung for 2–3 weeks.

REGION OF PRODUCTION:
SCOTLAND.

Haggis

DESCRIPTION:

A COOKED PUDDING OF SHEEP'S PLUCK IN A SHEEP'S STOMACH BAG: THE SHAPE AN OVAL MISSHAPEN BALL. WEIGHT: FROM 75–100G (INDIVIDUAL SIZE) TO 4–5KG ('CHIEFTAIN' HAGGIS TO FEED 20); THE MEAN IS 250–500G. COLOUR: GREYISH-CREAM. FLAVOUR: PEPPERY, SOMETIMES WITH A STRONG LIVER TASTE.

HISTORY:

Though the habit of cooking the entrails of an animal stuffed into the stomach bag has an ancient ancestry, at least as far back as Roman cookery, the haggis's development in Britain has taken some curious twists. The word itself is English, not exclusively Scottish, its derivation unknown. There are plenty of medieval and early-modern English references to establish it was a dish eaten throughout Britain – especially in the highland zones where oatmeal was an acceptable grain. It was not always made with sheep's pluck. Calf and pig are mentioned by Gervase Markham (1615). Robert May (1660) devotes a section to 'Sheeps Haggas Puddings', and includes a fast-day version as well as one made with calf's paunch and innards. The dish also figures in much later English dialect glossaries, for example from Northumberland and Gloucestershire, but at some point in the eighteenth century, it begins to be perceived as specifically Caledonian. Hannah Glasse (1747) refers to 'Scotch haggass' (although suggesting it be made with calf's pluck) and Smollett writes in *Humphrey Clinker* (1771), 'I am not yet Scotchman enough to relish their singed sheep's-head and haggice.'

Around this time, Scotland's poet Robert Burns wrote his 'Address to a Haggis'. Drawing attention to the charms and usefulness of bringing together the odds and ends of offal in an economical 'Great Chieftain o' the Puddin race', he turned the humble haggis into a symbol of Scottish sense of worth. After his death in 1796, the Edinburgh literati honoured his memory with a supper where the haggis was piped in by a piper and addressed with Burns' poem in a ritual procedure. Burns' Suppers have continued to be celebrated every year around 25 January, the poet's birthday, and the haggis has become inextricably linked with Scotland and Burns. Today it is made by all Scottish butchers and several meat-processing companies to meet a year-round demand.

The ingredients have varied over the years. Fifteenth-century recipes use the liver and blood of the sheep, while later, in the 1600s, a meatless 'Haggas Pudding in a Sheep's Paunch' requires a highly seasoned mixture of oatmeal, beef suet, and onions; it was sewn up and boiled, and served after cutting a hole in the top to be filled with butter melted with two eggs. Another recipe uses a calf's paunch and entrails, minced with bread, egg yolks, cream, spices, dried fruits and herbs, served as a sweet with sugar and almonds. Meg Dods (1826) has what she calls a finer haggis, 'made by parboiling and skinning sheep's tongues and kidneys, and substituting these minced, for most of the lights [lungs], and soaked bread or crisped crumbs for the toasted meal [oatmeal]'.

Among professional haggis-makers there is some controversy about the correct ingredients, since not all use a sheep's pluck of liver, heart and lights (lungs) but add other meats, or pig or ox liver – deemed by purists to produce a haggis without the real 'haggis-flavour'. These recipes are closely guarded secrets. The recent winner of a competition remarked that his had come from an old butcher he had worked for who had only relinquished his recipe under pressure when on the point of retirement.

Haggis may be served in its skin with mashed potatoes and mashed turnip ('tatties and neeps'), or with clapshot (mashed potatoes and turnip mixed together). To reheat, it should be wrapped in foil and baked in the oven. 'Haggis meat,' said Meg Dods, 'for those who do not admire the natural shape, may be poured out of the bag, and served in a deep dish.' It may also be made in a long sausage shape, sliced and fried or grilled.

Haggis is made by many craft butchers and several larger companies. It is sent through the mails to expatriate Scots throughout the world.

TECHNIQUE:

The pluck or innards (liver, heart and lungs) are washed and put to boil until tender. When cool, the meat is chopped or minced finely and mixed with oatmeal (which may be pinhead, coarse or medium), onions, salt, pepper and spices. It is again put through a coarser mincer. The mixture is moistened, usually with meat gravy, and pumped into prepared natural or artificial casings which are then sealed. The haggis is boiled in water for about an hour, depending on size. The filling is always rather loose as it swells up to fill the skins during boiling.

REGION OF PRODUCTION:

SCOTLAND.

Highland Cattle

DESCRIPTION:

AVERAGE DRESSED CARCASS WEIGHT FOR 26-MONTH STEER, 280KG. FLESH DARK RED, MARBLED WITH INTRA-MUSCULAR CREAM FAT; LEAN EXTERNAL FAT. DEEP-FLAVOURED MEAT BECAUSE OF MATURITY; AT ITS BEST WHEN IT HAS BEEN HUNG 2–3 WEEKS.

HISTORY:

Before the Jacobite Rebellion of 1745, native Highland cattle were an important part of the clan-based economy. Used as a supply of milk, cheese and butter, the dairy cows were driven in the summer months to the mountain pastures. The women and children of the clan moved with them to live in sheilings (dwellings in the hills).

'Better is a dinner of herbs where love is, than a stalled ox and hatred therewith.'

PROVERBS, 15:17

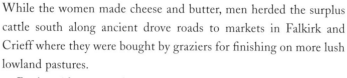

While the women made cheese and butter, men herded the surplus cattle south along ancient drove roads to markets in Falkirk and Crieff where they were bought by graziers for finishing on more lush lowland pastures.

By the mid-nineteenth century the trade had reduced, partly on the break-up of the clan system following the Highland Clearances, partly because of demand for better quality beef. Those early cattle were often 4–5 years old, their carcasses did not provide the same tender meat as young beasts reared and fattened nearer the market on the new fodder crops.

Although in commercial decline, the breed was encouraged by certain lairds, notably the Stewart brothers of Harris, McNeil of Bara, and the Dukes of Hamilton and Argyll. Stock was selected from island and Highland populations, with no evidence of lowland blood. The breed society was founded in 1884 with 516 bulls listed in the first herd book. Most were black or dun. Some exports went to Canada in 1882 and, in the 1920s, more were made to the USA and South America. Now there has been a revival of interest, particularly for the quality of the lean meat. Butchers who specialize in pure Highland beef attract a loyal following.

TECHNIQUE:

Hardiness has remained a key characteristic of this breed. Like the Aberdeen-Angus, it is related to the Galloway. There is a common ancestry of primitive native stock. The Highland can survive well on rough mountain pasture with some additional feeding in winter. Because of their hardiness and very long, thick coats they withstand extreme cold and thrive outside during the winter.

REGION OF PRODUCTION:

SCOTLAND.

Jellied Tripe

DESCRIPTION:

TRIPE, ONIONS, MILK, FLOUR AND SEASONINGS SET IN VARYING SIZES OF PLASTIC POT. COLOUR: CREAMY-WHITE IF MADE WITH BLEACHED TRIPE. FLAVOUR: A STRONG ONION TASTE, USUALLY WELL PEPPERED. MAY ALSO BE SET IN JELLIED COOKING LIQUOR WITHOUT THICKENING OR ONIONS.

HISTORY:

Tripe suppers were a feature of Edinburgh taverns through the eighteenth and well into the nineteenth centuries, supplied with plentiful quantities of cleaned tripe from the flesh- market. It was put in cutlet-sized pieces into a huge earthenware jar along with a knuckle bone or cowheel. The jar was covered and put into a cauldron of hot water and left at the side of the fire, just simmering, for about a day. The bone was removed, the contents left to set to a firm jelly then kept in a cool larder for future use. Scots were adventurous with their tripe, described in Meg Dods (1826) as evidence of 'good old French cookery', when the tripe was stewed in its liquor with herbs, onions, chives, wine, tarragon and mustard, the sauce thickened with flour.

During the twentieth century, their sense of adventure perhaps moderated. Included in the diet of the urban working classes as a cheap, sustaining meal, tripe's image deteriorated as it became associated with poverty and deprivation and a method of cooking which did not always enhance its qualities. It survives because of *aficionados* who have not only the cooking skills to make the most of its plebeian qualities, but also the sense not to be snobbish about its origins. Jellied tripe is brought home from the butcher's, then is reheated and eaten with boiled floury potatoes.

TECHNIQUE:

For the flour-thickened version, a white sauce is made with onions and the pre-cooked tripe, cut into small pieces, is added. It is poured into moulds and left to set. For the jellied version: the pre-cooked tripe is set in jellied stock without added gelatine or aspic. The tripe was originally unbleached.

Lorne Sausage

DESCRIPTION:

AN UNCASED, UNCOOKED, FRESH BEEF SAUSAGE WITH A SQUARE SECTION. CUT FROM A LARGE BLOCK AND SOLD IN SLICES APPROXIMATELY 10CM SQUARE, 1CM THICK. COLOUR: PINK. FLAVOUR: BEEF.

HISTORY:

This became associated in Glasgow with the comedian Tommy Lorne, a popular music-hall performer of the decades between the world wars who often made rude jokes about the Glasgow square sausage describing it as a 'doormat'. It was an important part of the urban eating habits of industrialised Scotland but remains popular. Known only in Glasgow as a Lorne sausage, the rest of the country refers to it as a square or sliced sausage. Its square, flat shape is a convenient fit for a morning roll along with a fried egg. The use of beef reflects the less prominent place that pig meat has in Scottish food habits.

TECHNIQUE:

Beef and fat in equal quantities are minced together and mixed with binder, seasonings and water. The mixture is then pressed into a Lorne tin (38cm long by 10cm at the top edge, tapering to 8cm at the base and holding 2kg of mixture). The surface is pressed by hand and the tin inverted on a tray immediately and the sausage turned out. It is left to set and harden in the refrigerator for several hours before slicing to order.

REGION OF PRODUCTION:

SCOTLAND.

Potted Hough

DESCRIPTION:

JELLIED MEAT (USUALLY BEEF) SET IN A POT, 125–250G. COLOUR: GREYISH BROWN. FLAVOUR: STRONGLY BEEF, SOMETIMES HIGHLY PEPPERED AND SPICED.

HISTORY:

This is a useful by-product for butchers, using tough and sinewy meat by boiling it with bones to a jelly. It was an economy food that took advantage of household scraps and was once made in domestic kitchens, but is now almost exclusively commercially produced. Recipes from the late 1800s (McNeill, 1929) show Scottish potted meats as closer to the English brawn of jellied pig's head than to those meat pastes ground in a mortar once made in the country-house kitchens of the wealthy.

The word hough (-gh pronounce as the -ch in Bach) means shin. The dish has extended its purview to take in similar bits of the animal such as head meat, knuckle and other bones. Some of this, although not all, is first pickled in brine. An alternative name in some butchers' shops is potted heid (head).

Hough became especially popular among the city poor, where it made a cheap meal with toast and tea. Today, in large housing schemes on the outskirts of towns, an independent butcher might make 15kg a week. Primarily a summer food, it is always eaten cold, often with pickled beetroot or salad.

TECHNIQUE:

Hough (shin of beef), head meat and bones are boiled for 6–12 hours. Mace and cloves are sometimes added. The pot is left to set overnight and fat which has risen and hardened can be removed. The meat is minced finely and the stock strained. They are mixed, seasoned and poured into wetted moulds.

REGION OF PRODUCTION:

SCOTLAND.

Scotch Pies

DESCRIPTION:

A ROUND, RAISED PIE OF COOKED BEEF OR MUTTON, GENERALLY 9CM DIAMETER, BUT SMALLER ONES (5CM ACROSS) ARE ALSO MADE. THE HEIGHT IS 3.5–4CM TO THE TOP EDGE, WHICH EXTENDS (BY ABOUT 1CM) BEYOND THE ROUND OF PASTRY WHICH COVERS THE FILLING, MAKING A CENTRAL SPACE FOR HOLDING 'FILLINGS' OR GRAVY. COLOUR: PALE GOLD, THE TOP EDGE USUALLY DARKER GOLD TO DARK BROWN. FLAVOUR: SOMETIMES QUITE PEPPERY.

HISTORY:

The pie (which is an English word of no certain derivation) was not indigenous to Scotland. At one critical juncture, it was identified as a luxurious, immoral introduction from dissolute England. In 1430, some years after the return of King James I from exile south of the border, his subjects were upbraided by the Bishop of St Andrews for their 'wicked usage' and adoption of the manners of the sophisticated English. The consequence was a self-denying ordinance – a reduction in the elaboration of meals in the country at large. Only the gentry, henceforth, and only on feast days, would be served pies: 'this use of them not being knowne in Scotland till that season' (Allen, 1994).

Scotch pies, once also commonly known as mutton pies, are descendants of these fifteenth-century villains: a raised pie made with hot-water paste coaxed up the side of a mould, then left to set and harden before the filling, is added. It is manufactured in a size suitable for a single serving. Its popularity appears to have developed in the latter part of the nineteenth century as industrialization brought large numbers of people into cities, where wages were low and living (and cooking) conditions poor. Made by local bakers, itinerant pie-men or -women or by tavern cooks, the 'hot-pie' ('het-pey' in Dundee) became a sustaining convenience food for workers. They had to be eaten hot: either hot from the bakers, or reheated at home. Some bakers who provided the 'hot-pie' service also kept a jug of hot gravy for pouring into the centre of the pie. Tinned beans and mashed potatoes became popular 'fillers' piled up in the space above the meat.

At first, the pie was always minced mutton, making use of tough, mature meat unsuitable for other purposes. This has largely been superseded today by beef. McNeill (1929) quotes a St Andrews professor describing the pies of his childhood which were made by the pie-wife: 'Delightful as were her pigeon and apple pies, her chef-d'oeuvre … was a certain kind of mutton-pie. The mutton was minced to the smallest consistency, and was made up in standing crust, which was strong enough to contain the most delicious gravy … There were no lumps of fat or grease in them at all … They always arrived piping hot … It makes my mouth water still when I think of those pies.'

On the West Coast, the most renowned pie-maker was also a woman, known as 'Granny Black', whose tavern in the Candleriggs in Glasgow became Mecca for pie-lovers around the early 1900s.

Though sold today from all bakeries on a daily basis, the hot-pie trade moves into mass-production on Saturdays as they are delivered to football grounds for eating at half-time – with a cup of hot Bovril. An average-sized baker's, with a football ground to supply on a Saturday, could make 35,000 pies each week.

Smaller, half-size pies are made by a few bakers. The range of fillings has now extended beyond plain and simple minced beef. Some are made with onion; others are still filled with mutton as of old; some have chopped beef steak rather than mince, when they are described as steak pies; more adventurous concoctions may be suitable for vegetarians, perhaps a custard of cheese and tomato, macaroni cheese, or vegetables in a savoury custard. These last are mostly baked without the pastry lids.

TECHNIQUE:

A hot-water paste is made, but using beef dripping instead of the lard – rendered pig fat – used in England. The proportion of flour to fat is relatively high, about 4:1; this is shaped in the pie-moulding machine before it cools. The pie shells are left overnight to harden. The meat is prepared and seasoned with salt, pepper and other spices such as mace or nutmeg; this is used to fill the cases about half-full. The lids are placed on top and the pies baked in a very hot oven for 15–20 minutes.

REGION OF PRODUCTION:
SCOTLAND.

Abernethy Biscuit

DESCRIPTION:
A THIN, ROUND, FLAT BISCUIT PRICKED ON TOP, 65–85MM DIAMETER. WEIGHT: 15G. COLOUR: PALE GOLD. FLAVOUR AND TEXTURE: A SEMI-SWEET, CRISP BISCUIT BUT CONTAINING LESS BUTTER AND SUGAR THAN SHORTBREAD, ORIGINALLY FLAVOURED WITH CARAWAY.

HISTORY:
Before the Norse invasions Abernethy (Tayside) was the seat of Pictish kings. The banal explanation of these biscuits' name is that they emanated from the eponymous burgh (Simon, 1960). A more fanciful tale suggests they are named for a surgeon, Dr John Abernethy (d. 1831), an ornament of St Bartholomew's Hospital in London. He had the habit of taking a lunchtime snack at the nearby baker's of hard captain's or ship's biscuits. Abernethy is reputed to have suggested to the baker, John Caldwell, that the biscuits might be more palatable with the addition of some sugar and caraway. As a result the new biscuit became very popular and Caldwell named them after his customer. How the recipe made the jump from London to Scotland is not explained. Abernethy himself was educated at Wolverhampton Grammar School and died at his home in Enfield, not a Scot at all.

Early recipes, for example Cassell (1896), Bond (1923) and Simon (1960), are for a dry biscuit with no more than an ounce of butter and sugar to a pound of flour. Modern recipes call for more fat and sugar and no flavouring with the caraway which was once universal.

TECHNIQUE:
Domestic recipes are based on 250g flour to 75g of both sugar and

butter to 1 teaspoon baking powder, 1 egg, 1 tablespoon milk and 1 teaspoon caraway seeds. The method involves mixing the dry ingredients, rubbing in the butter and mixing with the egg and milk to make a stiff dough. When rolled out, the centres are pricked with a fork and they are baked in a moderately hot oven for about 10 minutes. Commercial recipes are simpler, using only flour, sugar, fat, baking powder, salt and water, without caraway seeds.

REGION OF PRODUCTION:
SCOTLAND.

Bap

DESCRIPTION:

A SOFT ROLL, USUALLY ROUND, SOMETIMES OVAL OR TRIANGULAR; AN ABERDEEN BAP IS SQUARISH; FLAT-TOPPED AND FLOURY, SOMETIMES WITH A SINGLE INDENTATION IN THE MIDDLE TO PREVENT IT RISING TO A DOME. COLOUR: WHITE OR LIGHT BROWN UNDER A DUSTING OF FLOUR. FLAVOUR: SALTY.

HISTORY:

Bap is the Scots word for a soft morning roll. It is also known as floury bap, a simple reference to its dusting of flour. The origin of the word is obscure. McNeill (1929) suggests an analogy with pap, the Scots word for the mammary gland, because of its shape and size. Their first identified mention is in account rolls of the sixteenth century, and there are several references in later printed sources, for example Alan Ramsay's *Tea-table Miscellany* (1724-7). The word was a generic description (much as loaf is of bread), therefore the size and shape of baps has been extremely varied. A shearer's or harvester's bap, taken out into the fields at midday, was the size of a large meat plate (McNeill, 1929). Dean Ramsay's *Reminiscences of Scottish Life and Character* (1858) includes the question, 'Are ye for our burial baps round or square?' Another source confirms the truth: 'The grandfather of the late Prime Minister of Great Britain [W.E. Gladstone] kept a shop in Leith Walk in Edinburgh,

where he sold "baps", flour, oatmeal, peas, etc., and where he was popularly known to the boys of the neighbour-hood as "Sma' Baps", because his baps were reputed to be smaller than those of his brother tradesmen' (Mackay, 1888).

Although softer in texture and crust, the bap fulfilled the same function for many Scots as the Glasgow roll (see above, p. 313): it was used as an envelope for a filling. Baps are split in half through the middle and buttered rather than broken up to eat. MacClure (1955) describes his earliest (and best) recollection: 'having it stuffed with Ayrshire bacon and a fried egg to eat while hastening to beat the bell for morning school … On these occasions it was still warm from the baker's oven.'

TECHNIQUE:

MacClure (1955) gives instructions for a bap: 'sift a pound of flour into a warmed bowl with a teaspoonful of salt, and you lightly rub in two ounces of lard. On the side in another bowl, you mix an ounce of yeast with a teaspoon of sugar until they become liquid, then you add half-a-pint of tepid water-and-milk mixed in equal proportions. This warmish liquid you strain into the flour, obtaining a soft dough. You cover this dough with a cloth, and leave it in a warm place for about an hour so that it will rise. Then you lightly knead your dough, which you divide into oval pieces, say about four-and-a-half inches long by about three wide. This makes a man-size bap. One hears of glazed baps, but they are unorthodox. 'Floury baps' are the thing. You brush the tops with milk, as if to give a glaze, but you immediately dust them with flour, which you repeat just before you place them in the oven. But before doing this last, you place the baps on a greased and floured oven-tray, and leave them for quarter-of-an-hour or so to prove. To stop the baps from blistering, you press a finger in their centres just before they go into the oven. This last should be fairly hot, and about twenty minutes should bake the man-size bap. The bap should go warm to the breakfast table.'

REGION OF PRODUCTION:

SCOTLAND.

Clootie Dumpling

DESCRIPTION:

A PUDDING STEAMED IN A CLOTH (CLOOT) — A ROUND, FLATTENED BALL-LIKE SHAPE, MORE CURVED AND ROUNDED ON THE UPPER SIDE WITH A SHINY LEATHER-LIKE SKIN, OFTEN SOLD CUT IN SLICES. A WHOLE DUMPLING WEIGHS APPROXIMATELY 900G (LARGE), 680G (MEDIUM), OR 113G (SMALL). COLOUR: LIGHT BROWN ON OUTSIDE, DARKER INSIDE, DEPTH OF COLOUR DEPENDS ON AMOUNT OF SPICES AND BLACK TREACLE. FLAVOUR AND TEXTURE: SPICY, SWEET, FRUITY.

HISTORY:

This pudding developed as a sweet version of the savoury pudding (haggis) stuffed into sheep's or pig's stomach bags and boiled in a large cauldron. Using instead a cotton or linen cloth, the sweet pudding mixture was made originally as the Scottish alternative to a baked celebration fruit cake for holidays, birthdays and during winter solstice celebrations, known in Scotland as the Daft Days.

Easily made in the common domestic setting where there was no oven and the cooking was done solely over a fire in a large pot, these special-occasion dumplings usually contained a selection of 'surprises': a ring signifying marriage, a coin — wealth, a button — bachelorhood, a thimble — spinsterhood, a wishbone — the heart's desire, a horse-shoe — good luck. Compared with rich celebration fruit cakes, or an English Christmas pudding, the dumpling mixture is much plainer. No hard and fast rules apply to the degree of richness, or even to the exact content since it has always been a rule-of-thumb affair, depending largely on the fortunes of the family.

Clootie dumpling is served with custard, cream or a bowl of soft brown sugar. When cold it is often fried with bacon and eggs for breakfast. Unlike Christmas pudding tradition south of the border it does not have the same strict linkage to mid-winter feasting.

TECHNIQUE:

A typical recipe is 125g self-raising flour, 175g fine white breadcrumbs, 125g beef suet, 2 teaspoons baking powder, 2 teaspoons each of freshly

These much-loved Scotch pancakes are small and thickish, served for tea with butter and jam. They were very much a part of my childhood, flipped over on the girdle as I came home from school. Traditionally Scotch pancakes are, of course, made on a girdle (griddle). If you have never used one before, it is easy: you can test it is hot enough by dropping a teaspoonful of the batter on to the surface. It should set almost at once – and, if it begins to bubble after one minute, the girdle is ready. The large bubbles tell you the pancakes are ready to be flipped over.

You can substitute the same amount of self-raising flour for the plain flour/cream of tartar/bicarbonate of soda combination, or use half buckwheat flour and half plain flour (omitting the sugar and adding a pinch of salt) to make cheat's blinis. Serve these with a horseradish cream made by combining a small tub of sour cream or crème fraiche with enough horseradish to taste. Spread this on to the pancakes then top with smoked salmon, caviar or herring roe and a snip of chives.

Sue Lawrence

FROM SUE LAWRENCE'S *BOOK OF BAKING*

Scotch Pancakes

Makes 12-16

115G/4OZ/1 CUP PLAIN FLOUR, SIFTED

½ TEASPOON CREAM OF TARTAR

¼ TEASPOON BICARBONATE OF SODA

1 TEASPOON GOLDEN CASTER SUGAR

1 MEDIUM FREE RANGE EGG

150ML/5FL OZ/2/3 CUP OF MILK

MELTED BUTTER FOR GREASING

Sift the flour, cream of tartar and bicarbonate of soda into a bowl and stir in the sugar. Add the egg and slowly add the milk, whisking all the time with a balloon whisk. Whisk until smooth.

Heat up a girdle (griddle) or frying pan; it will take at least three minutes. Once hot, smear with a little butter, then drop in four tablespoons of the batter to cook four pancakes at a time. After one and a half minutes you will see large bubbles. Flip the pancakes over and continue to cook for a further one minute or so until just done. Serve Warm.

ground cinnamon, ginger and nutmeg, 175g sultanas, 175g California raisins, 2 tablespoons Golden Syrup, 2 tablespoons black treacle, 2 eggs, 1 large cooking apple, grated, 1 large carrot, grated, and milk to mix. Use a cotton or linen cloth 550mm square. To prepare the pot and cloth, fill a large pot with water, place a metal grid or upside-down saucer in the base. Bring to the boil and put in the cloth for a few minutes. Lift out with tongs and spread on a table. Sprinkle with plain flour, shake off excess. Put all the ingredients into a large bowl (add trinkets wrapped in greaseproof paper) and mix to a fairly stiff consistency with orange juice. Put in the centre of the cloth, bring up edges and tie with string, leaving space for expansion. Hold up the tied ends and pat the dumpling into a good round shape. Place in simmering water which should come about halfway up the dumpling, and simmer for 4 hours. Fill a large bowl with cold water. Lift out the dumpling and plunge into the cold water. Keep submerged for about a minute and this will release the cloth from the pudding skin. Put into a bowl about the same size as the dumpling, untie the string, open out the cloth, place the serving-dish on top and reverse. Peel off the cloth and dry out the outer 'skin' in a warm place. Serve with sweetened double cream.

REGION OF PRODUCTION:
SCOTLAND.

Petticoat Tails

DESCRIPTION:
A SHORTBREAD BISCUIT BAKED IN A ROUND RESEMBLING THAT OF AN OUTSPREAD BELL-HOOP CRINOLINE PETTICOAT – WITH A SMALL CIRCLE CUT OUT OF THE CENTRE. THE BISCUIT IS THEN MARKED OR CUT INTO SEGMENTS. BECAUSE OF THE REMOVAL OF THE INNER CIRCLE, THERE IS NO LONGER A POINTED END TO EACH WEDGE OF BISCUIT, THUS AVOIDING UNTIDY BREAKAGE IN THE CRISP, CRUMBLY SHORTBREAD.

HISTORY:
There are several possible, and fanciful, explanations of the name.

Hartley (1954) suggests they were originally called, in the twelfth century, *petty* [little] *cotes* [a small enclosure] *tallis* [a cut-out pattern from the cuts on sticks made for measuring or tallying]. This evolved into *petticote tallis* when the central round was removed and the biscuits formed the pattern of women's gored skirts or petticoats. Another theory is that it could be a corruption of the French *petites gatelles*, which were small French cakes popular with Mary, Queen of Scots, who is said to have brought them from France in 1560. However, *The Annals of The Cleikum Club*, the leading nineteenth-century gastronomic club, opined that 'in Scottish culinary terms there are many corruptions, though we rather think the name petticoat tails has its origin in the shape of the cakes, which is exactly that of the bell-hoop petticoats of our ancient Court ladies'.

Around the time of the Cleikum Club, Meg Dods (1829) wrote: 'Scotch petticoat-tails: Mix a half-ounce of caraway-seeds with the fourth of a peck of flour. Make a hole in the middle of the flour, and pour into it twelve ounces of butter melted in a quarter pint of milk, and three ounces of beat sugar. Knead this, but not too much, or it will become tough; divide it into two, and roll it out round rather thin. Cut out the cake by running a paste-cutter round a dinner pate, or any large round plate. Cut a cake from the centre of this one with a small saucer or large tumbler. Keep this inner circle whole, but cut the outer one into eight petticoat tails. Bake all these on paper laid on tins, serve the round cake in the middle of the plate, and the petticoat-tails as radii round it.'

Today the differences between shortbread and petticoat tails are shape, thickness and texture. Though some producers make both from the same mixture, others make a less gritty, softer, more melting biscuit for petticoat tails. Shortbread manufacturers have exploited the distinctive shape, treating it as a luxury requiring special packaging.

TECHNIQUE:

Although the proportions of flour, butter and sugar are the same as shortbread (approximately 6:4:2), those producers who make a distinction between the texture of shortbread and petticoat tails replace some of the flour with cornflour and some of the sugar with icing sugar. The method is to mix the butter and sugar together and then work them into the flour to make a firm, pliable dough which is rolled out and shaped. It is baked in a slow oven (150°C) until uniformly pale, golden brown.

REGION OF PRODUCTION:
SCOTLAND.

Scone

DESCRIPTION:

GIRDLE AND OVEN SCONES ARE ROUND OR TRIANGULAR (FARL) IN SHAPE; SODA GIRDLE SCONES ARE APPROXIMATELY 150MM ROUNDS, OTHER SCONES ARE 50–70MM DIAMETER. COLOUR: FROM DARK BROWN (MADE WITH TREACLE) TO FLOURY-WHITE.

POTATO SCONES: A FARL (TRIANGULAR) SHAPE IS MOST COMMON, BUT THEY ARE OCCASIONALLY ROUND, 100–150MM ACROSS, ABOUT 5MM THICK. THEY ARE MOTTLED ON THE SURFACE, CREAM OR WHITE INSIDE; THEIR FLAVOUR IS UNSWEETENED, SALTY, REDOLENT OF POTATO AND THEIR TEXTURE IS SMOOTH.

HISTORY:

This is a composite entry for 2 distinct varieties of a single Scottish food type. A scone is a small round piece of dough, more or less enriched and cooked either upon a girdle – a flat iron plate heated on the flame – or baked in an oven. They may be made with barley or wheaten flour, or have an addition of potato. They may be chemically leavened or, in the case of barley, not leavened at all.

The word scone appears to have been adopted first by the Scots though it is also common in England. Scots pronounce it with a short vowel as in 'gone' while the southern English pronunciation is usually with a diphthong rhyming with 'stone'. The word is thought to have been adopted from the Dutch *schoonbrot* meaning fine white bread.

The poet Robert Burns refers to them as 'souple [soft] scones, the wale [choicest] of food'. It is most likely his would have been made with barley meal, cooked to a porridge with water and salt, then small spoonfuls removed from the pan, pressed out on a board floured with barley meal and fired on both sides on the girdle until browned – a method described in Clark (1909). What he was referring to was not the soft, baking-powder scone common today, but to the pliability or suppleness which is still the criterion for a good potato scone. The softness was a notable change from hard-tack oatcakes.

The fugitives who 'lay upon the bare top of a rock, like scones upon a girdle,' in Robert Louis Stevenson's *Kidnapped* would have found themselves in the transitional period, between old-fashioned thin barley-meal scones, baked on the girdle, and oven scones. Modern bakers have transferred most, but not all, scones to the oven. Despite this, the demand for girdle-baked scones continues and every Scottish baker has a large hot-plate where daily he girdle-bakes a supply of soda scones, potato scones, pancakes and crumpets. When English supermarket chains started putting in-store bakeries into their Scottish branches, they were obliged to put in hot-plates for girdle-baking. Although early scones were yeast-raised, most of those now produced and eaten in Scotland and the rest of Britain are chemically aerated.

Scones baked in the oven, using wheaten flour and raised with chemical agents, developed as the Scots population acquired baking powder in the 1860s and baking ovens became a more common domestic appliance. With the appearance of a new commercial form – the tea-room – in Glasgow around the same time, these scones became a tea-bread item presented to customers on the decorative 3-tiered stand. Freshly baked scones were essential daily fare for both afternoon and high teas, spread with butter and jam. Modern oven scones comprise the whole gamut of base materials and added flavours or ingredients. They may be made with wheaten flour (wholemeal or white), oatmeal or barley meal, butter or buttermilk, soured milk or fresh milk, treacle, honey, cream, herbs, spices, nuts, dates, fruit or cheese. Although Scotland is properly their region of origin, oven scones are now baked throughout Britain. Few English people would appreciate that this was as Scottish as oatmeal porridge.

It is not clear when the habit of baking scones with mashed potato added to the flour developed. They were certainly known in the 1930s when the novelist Dorothy L. Sayers addressed a foreword in one of her books to a Scottish hotel keeper, remarking that she would 'come back next summer for some more potato scones'. They are also colloquially known as tattie scones. Potato scones are sold in packets, from groceries as well as bakeries, and may be heated and rolled with butter and jam for tea, or fried with bacon for breakfast.

TECHNIQUE:

For girdle scones, the butter is rubbed into the flour and raising agents, and the ingredients mixed to a soft dough with fresh milk (if baking powder) or buttermilk (if baking soda). It is shaped into a large round marked into triangles or cut into individual scones. A scone is distinguished from the large round bannock by its size and shape.

For oven scones, mixing and shaping may be the same as for girdle scones. They are baked in a hot oven (230°C) for 15–20 minutes.

For potato scones, butter is melted with the potatoes which are mashed and mixed into the flour with milk to make a stiff dough. This is rolled out to a large thin round the size of a meat plate, marked into triangles and baked on both sides on a hot girdle.

REGION OF PRODUCTION:
SCOTLAND.

Scottish Cookie

DESCRIPTION:

A ROUND BUN, 90MM DIAMETER, 40–50MM HIGH. COLOUR AND TEXTURE: GOLDEN EGG-GLAZED SURFACE, PALE YELLOWISH, OPEN-TEXTURED INTERIOR. FLAVOUR: YEASTY, SLIGHTLY SWEET.

HISTORY:

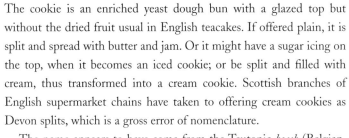

The cookie is an enriched yeast dough bun with a glazed top but without the dried fruit usual in English teacakes. If offered plain, it is split and spread with butter and jam. Or it might have a sugar icing on the top, when it becomes an iced cookie; or be split and filled with cream, thus transformed into a cream cookie. Scottish branches of English supermarket chains have taken to offering cream cookies as Devon splits, which is a gross error of nomenclature.

The name appears to have come from the Teutonic *koeck* (Belgian, *koekie*; Dutch, *koekje*), the diminutive of cake. There are various references to cookies over the last 300 years: for example a 'cukie' is mentioned in domestic accounts of the seventeenth century and Sir Walter Scott in The *Antiquary* writes, 'Muckle [much] obliged to ye for your cookies, Mrs Shortcake.' A later appearance is by R.M. Williamson in 1929: 'I want a plain ham and egg tea, … and some cookies and cakes.' The Scots cookie joined other tea breads on the ornamental cake stands which decorated the centre of tables in Glasgow's innovative tea rooms at the turn of the last century. Originally privately owned, these were later taken over by bakery companies, who ran them until the beginning of the Second World War, selling a sophisticated range of Scottish baking including girdle-baked items like crumpets, pancakes and girdle scones which took their place usually on the middle tier. Cream and iced cookies were special treats on the top tier.

The Scottish cookie should not be confused with the flat, round biscuit which goes under the same name in North America.

TECHNIQUE:

A yeasted dough enriched with butter, milk and eggs. The cookies are baked for 10 minutes at 220°C. To make a cream cookie, the bun is split diagonally through the top, slightly to one side of the centre, and filled with piped cream. The whole surface is dusted with icing sugar.

REGION OF PRODUCTION:

SCOTLAND.

Scottish Crumpet

DESCRIPTION:

A ROUND BREAD PITTED WITH HOLES ON ONE SIDE AND A UNIFORM SURFACE ON THE OTHER; 120–150MM DIAMETER, 5MM HIGH. COLOUR: GOLDEN BROWN ON THE UNIFORM SURFACE, PALER ON THE LACY SURFACE. FLAVOUR AND TEXTURE: SWEET.

HISTORY:

The Scottish crumpet is thinner than both a girdle pancake or scone and the English bread that also goes under the name. The derivation is also unlike its southerly cousin. In the seventeenth century, there emerged a cake called the 'crompid cake', that is curled cake, from the verb to crump or crimp, because it curled or bent in the cooking on the girdle. Calling this a 'cake' was no more than the literal use of the word. Cakes were bread, distinguished either by their regularity of shape (and that they were not a great undistinguished loaf) or by their particular, sometimes fanciful, ingredients. The latter distinction is all that matters in modern usage. At first, it was the shape that counted most: thus oatcakes or pancakes, or the statement, 'Scotland is the land of cakes'.

Crumpets' development in Scotland may have a connection with the Shrove Tuesday pancake. It appears likely that they are a progression from the old Scottish car-cakes, mentioned by Sir Walter Scott in *The Bride of Lammermoor*. Car-cakes were made for Fastern's E'en (the Scottish equivalent of Shrove Tuesday) and are described in Jamieson's *Dictionary of the Scottish Language* (1818) as, 'a kind of thin cake, made of milk, meal or flour, eggs beaten up, and sugar'.

The Scots crumpet joined other tea-breads on the ornamental cake stands which decorated the centre of tea tables in Glasgow's tea rooms at the turn of the century. Girdle-baked items like crumpets, pancakes and girdle scones took their place on the middle tier.

TECHNIQUE:

The batter is more runny than for pancakes or drop scones and the crumpet is much the thinner when cooked. The ingredients and method of cooking, however, are the same as the Scottish pancake (see below).

Scottish Pancake

DESCRIPTION:

A DISC, UNIFORM ON BOTH SIDES, 70–90MM DIAMETER, 15MM HIGH. COLOUR: GOLDEN BROWN.

HISTORY:

This is known as a drop or dropped scone in England, and also sometimes in Scotland. The thick, aerated Scottish version should not be confused with a thin, unleavened English pancake. In Scottish bakeries today the description of pancake for the thick, aerated version is the one generally in use. This is a concept which has now been fairly well fixed in people's minds with the development of the similar (but much larger diameter) American thick pancakes featured in themed pancake-restaurants.

TECHNIQUE:

A thickish batter is mixed with flour, egg, sugar and either buttermilk and bicarbonate of soda or sweet milk and baking powder. It is poured in spoonfuls on a hot girdle and cooked for about 2 minutes, then turned and cooked for another minute. It is wrapped while warm to preserve its freshness. The pancake is a thicker item than the Scots crumpet and made with a thicker batter.

REGION OF PRODUCTION:

SCOTLAND.

Shortbread

DESCRIPTION:

MADE IN MANY SHAPES AND SIZES – SMALL AND LARGE ROUNDS, FINGERS AND WEDGES – THICKNESS 5–25MM. COLOUR: PALE, EVENLY GOLDEN. FLAVOUR AND TEXTURE: BUTTERY-SWEET; CRUMBLY TEXTURE VARYING FROM FINE TO COARSE.

'Kissing don't last: cookery do!'
GEORGE MEREDITH

The term short, used to describe a friable, brittle, crumbling texture, whether of food, soil or metal, has been applied since medieval times (*OED* quotes a cookery manuscript of *c.* 1430). Early examples in printed books include the short-paste that was made for Lent (*Good Huswife's Handmaide*, 1594) or the short paste as an alternative to puff paste used by Robert May (1660). Later the word was also prefixed to cake and bread. The first published Scottish cookery book, by Mrs McLintock (1736), says: 'To make Short Bread, Take a Peck of Flour, put three lb of Butter in among a little water, and let it melt, pout it in amongst your Flour, put in a Mutchkin of good Barm; when it is wrought divide it in 3 parts, roll out your cakes longer than broad, and gather from the sides with your Finger, cut through the Middle and job [jab, prick] it on Top, then send it to the oven.' By the 1850s, this yeast-leavened shortbread had been abandoned and the recipe modified to something more akin to modern style: a crumbling biscuit texture more befitting its description.

Although now an everyday food, it was originally a festive treat, flavoured and decorated accordingly. Meg Dods (1826) describes how she put more almonds and butter into a rich shortbread she intended to send 'as a holiday present to England'. Baked about an inch thick to withstand transport, this rich shortbread was flavoured with candied citron and orange peel and blanched almonds, the top strewn with caraway comfits. In time, it became known as a Pitcaithly Bannock, made originally by a woman in Pitcaithly (Perthshire). Besides its use as a present, it was also associated with the Yule season, embracing Christmas and Hogmanay, when thick round shortbread, a version of the old Yule bannock, was eaten.

Today, manufacturers continue to exploit shortbread's potential for flavour innovations by adding chocolate, ginger, almonds and so on. Some years ago the Scottish Association of Master Bakers was challenged by a government ruling threatening to classify shortbread as a common biscuit. Arguing rather that it was an item of flour confectionery, an amicable agreement was achieved and shortbread, though indeed eaten mostly as a common biscuit, retains its position as a special confection.

TECHNIQUE:

The ingredients are plain flour, including a small amount of rice flour for the gritty texture, butter and sugar in a ratio of 6:4:2 to make a firm but pliable dough which is rolled out and shaped. It is baked in a slow oven (150°C) until a pale golden brown.

REGION OF PRODUCTION:

SCOTLAND.

Square Loaf

DESCRIPTION:

A LOAF WITH STRAIGHT, SOFT SIDES AND CLOSE-TEXTURED CRUMB; ABOUT 190MM LONG, 60MM WIDE, 80MM TALL. COLOUR: DARK BROWN TO ALMOST BLACK ON TOP AND 'HEEL' END. FLAVOUR: SALTY.

HISTORY:

This loaf shape, also called plain loaf or batch bread, appears to have developed in the cities of Scotland during the industrialization of the late nineteenth and early twentieth centuries. The loaves were 'set so close together in the oven that they touch, in which case crumb instead of crust forms on the sides and the type becomes a crumby loaf' (Banfield, 1947). As modern bakers point out, it was an economical loaf to bake since the loaves rose upwards rather than outwards, giving their characteristic height. Banfield goes on to say that Scotland and Ireland have a 'strong penchant for bread so baked'. Though the loaf itself is not actually square, when a slice is cut in half it forms a square. It was a working-class, city alternative to the crusty country loaf and formed an important part of the diet.

A square loaf was a batch bread. The oven was charged with a group of loaves which touched as they expanded so that they were almost a single mass when cooked. This assured the lack of crust.

Because there was a limit to lateral expansion, the loaves rose much higher than bread that had space around it in the oven. This gave it the aerated texture increasingly favoured by the British. Other loaf shapes, for instance the cottage loaf and bloomer, might also be cooked on the batch principle – especially in urban bakeries with strong pressure of trade provoking high productivity and economic prudence. The square loaf may once have been baked on the sole of the oven, each piece of dough lovingly delivered there off the baker's peel. Nowadays, however, the baker is allowed to work in the cool of the kitchen to make up a large tin containing 24 loaves which can be loaded into the oven at once.

A variation on the square is a pan loaf. This is baked in a long tin with a tight-fitting lid. Each tin holds 4 loaves in a line. As they are put into the tin, the surface which touches its neighbour is brushed with fat. When the closed tin is placed in the oven, the rising dough fills it completely and the loaves are perfectly square when removed. The loaves are broken apart when cooled. The pan is a slightly richer bread, made originally with milk powder, sugar and butter (Banfield, 1947). The result is even softer and less crusty than a batch bread.

In city culture, a class distinction developed between those who ate 'plain' and those with aspirations, who ate 'pan'; a distinction which was transferred to speech, when 'pan-loaf' became a common term for those who deliberately changed their city vernacular accent into a more polished, sophisticated form.

These loaves were central to everyday life in Scotland for they were the perfect shape for lunch pieces (sandwiches) packed into square lunch boxes sometimes with a square sausage (see Lorne sausage, above). The Jeely (i.e. jam) 'Piece Song' (Adam McNaughton, *Noise and Smoky Breath*, 1983) describes them being also spread with jam and thrown out of tenement windows by mothers to their children playing in the back courts.

REGION OF PRODUCTION:
SCOTLAND.

Mixed Boilings

DESCRIPTION:

THIS IS A COLLECTION OF BOILED SWEETS, SOLD BY WEIGHT FROM A JAR WHICH CONTAINS A SELECTION OF THE FOLLOWING: BLACK-STRIPPIT (STRIPED) BALLS, A ROUND BALL WITH BLACK AND WHITE STRIPES, STRONGLY FLAVOURED WITH PEPPERMINT; SOOR PLOOMS [SOUR PLUMS], ROUND, BRIGHT GREEN, STRONGLY ACIDIC, LIME-FLAVOURED; ANISEED BALLS, ROUND, ANISEED FLAVOUR; HOREHOUND TOFFEES, USUALLY TRIANGULAR, FLAVOURED WITH ESSENCE OF WHITE HOREHOUND; CINNAMON BALLS, ROUND BALLS, FLAVOURED WITH OIL OF CINNAMON; BUTTERSCOTCH ROCK, SMALL BITE-SIZED PIECES, WITH A RICH BUTTER FLAVOUR; BARLEY SUGAR, A ROUND OR TRIANGULAR BOILING WITH A CLEAR GOLDEN SHINE; LIME ROCK, SHARPLY FLAVOURED; RHUBARB ROCK, SHOCKING PINK WITH A BRIGHT PALE GREEN CENTRE AND SHARP FLAVOUR; RUM TOFFEE, A HARD ROUND BALL, FLAVOURED WITH RUM. COMPOSITION: SUGAR, GLUCOSE, FLAVOURINGS, COLOURINGS.

HISTORY:

These bright mixtures have been made since at least the late nineteenth century. Craftsmen sugar-boilers and itinerant sweet-sellers provided a rich supply of colourful sweeties remembered by F.M. McNeill (1929): 'Besides such homely sweets as gundy, glessie, cheugh jeans and black man, there were bottles of "boilings" (Scotch mixtures) that glittered like rubies, emeralds and topazes and all the jewels of the Orient, and tasted of all the fruits of the orchard and spices of the Indies.' Many of the individual items within the mixtures have been known for as long as Scotland has had sweeties; barley sugar (along with tablet) is one of the earliest. It appears in Mrs McIver's list of Scottish National Dishes (1773), and was made originally with barley water (the water strained from cooking barley). Horehound, *Marrubium vulgare*, is a herb used as an ancient remedy for colds and coughs. Soor plooms have a legend attached: they were made to commemorate an incident in which a band of English marauders were surprised and routed when caught eating unripe plums in the Galashiels (Borders) area. Scottish mixed boilings are especially interesting because they reflect a taste for confectionery flavoured with spices (cloves, cinnamon and ginger all being commonly used) more or less vanished elsewhere in Britain.

Most Scottish confectioners offer at least one selection of mixed boilings and may do seasonal ones such as 'winter mixtures' of items considered especially warming like clove rock, aniseed balls, ginger drops, lemon rock and farmers' friends. Others offer variations such as 'mixed balls': striped round sweets in various colours and flavours.

A similar habit of selling mixed boiled sweets exists in parts of northern England, where they are known as 'Yorkshire Mixtures'; containing types of rock, mint balls, barley sugar, and fruit-flavoured drops in fish shapes.

TECHNIQUE:

There is little difference between the technique for boiled sweets and for mixed boilings. Sugar, water and glucose are boiled to 148–160°C, depending on the manufacturer and the exact nature of the confection. On removal from the heat, the sugar is poured on to a slab and divided into portions which are coloured and flavoured as required. For sweets such as black striped balls or rhubarb rock, some of the mixture is stretched or 'pulled' and used for striping the remainder of the batch before shaping into balls or sticks. For butterscotch, butter is added to the sugar during boiling.

REGION OF PRODUCTION:

SCOTLAND.

Tablet

DESCRIPTION:

SUGAR CANDY IN OBLONG BLOCKS 15–20MM THICK, MARKED INTO 30MM SQUARES. COLOUR: PALE TO DARK BROWN. FLAVOUR AND TEXTURE: VERY SWEET; CRISP BUT MELTING. COMPOSITION: SUGAR, THIN CREAM OR MILK,

SOMETIMES BUTTER. VARIANTS MAY CONTAIN CINNAMON, COCONUT, GINGER, LEMON, ORANGE, PEPPERMINT, VANILLA, WALNUT, CHOCOLATE.

HISTORY:

First used as a sweet vehicle for sour medicines, medicinal tablets were made by apothecaries in both England and Scotland. The term was abandoned in England but continued in Scotland, transferring to an item of confectionery as sugar from the West Indies became plentiful in the nineteenth century. Earlier entries have referred to Scotland's distinctive confectionery but tablet has arguably the longest history. Certainly it is now the most widely made, with national rather than regional repute. Early documentation is in the household book of Lady Grisell Baillie (1692–1733) referring to 'taiblet for the bairns'.

While Grisell Baillie was buying tablet for her children, Mrs McLintock, author of the first published Scottish cookery book, was writing recipes for 'tablets'. To make Orange Tablets with the Grate [zest]; To make Rose Tablets; To make Ginger Tablets; and To make Cinnamon Tablets: 'Take half an ounce of cinnamon, beat and search [sieve] it, or take four Guts [drops] of the Spirit of Cinnamon [distilled bruised cinnamon and rose water] to a pound of sugar; take half a mutchkin of water, clarify it with the white of an egg, put it on a slow fire, and boil it till it be almost candy'd and put in the four Guts of the Spirit of Cinnamon, mix them well together, rub the papers wither with sweet oil or fresh butter and pour it out, and cut them in small four corner's pieces.'

Today tablet is distinguished from fudge by its crisp bite. The degree of bite depends on the richness of the ingredients. Tablet has less butter and glucose than fudge; it is also boiled to a slightly lower temperature.

TECHNIQUE:

Sugar, water, single cream and/or milk (sometimes condensed milk), butter (commercial makers also add glucose and/or fondant while some domestic recipes suggest syrup or vinegar) are boiled to 115°C (soft ball). While still hot, the mixture is beaten until it begins to grain slightly. It is poured into a buttered tray and left until just set before marking into small squares.

REGION OF PRODUCTION:
SCOTLAND.

Grain and Blended Whisky

DESCRIPTION:

WHISKY IS A DISTILLED LIQUOR MADE FROM BARLEY, MALTED FOR MALT WHISKY, BUT NOT FOR GRAIN. EACH HAS ITS DISCRETE MANUFACTURING PROCESS AS WELL AS RAW INGREDIENT. A GRAIN WHISKY HAS A QUIETER PERSONALITY WHICH MAKES IT OFTEN, THOUGH NOT ALWAYS, LESS INTERESTING THAN A MALT. A BLENDED WHISKY IS A BLEND OF BOTH MALT AND GRAIN WHISKIES. IN COLOUR THEY VARY FROM PALE TO DARK GOLD AND ARE USUALLY AROUND 40 PER CENT PROOF. MOST GRAIN WHISKY IS USED TO SOFTEN AND LIGHTEN A BLEND AND THERE ARE ONLY 2 COMPANIES WHICH PUT STATED-AGE SINGLE GRAINS IN A BOTTLE.

HISTORY:

Grain whisky developed after the invention in 1832, by Irishman Aeneas Coffey, of the patent still which allowed distillation to take place in a continuous process in a single still. Whisky could be produced more cheaply but the method yielded a less characterful result than the malted-grain whiskies made in the pot still.

In the 1850s, however, the face of the industry was changed when the Edinburgh merchant, Andrew Usher, who was the agent for Glenlivet, vatted together several casks from his stocks, producing a more consistent product. Vatting was soon extended to the blending of malt and grain, producing a lighter spirit which the English, unused to the much stronger malt, found more palatable. This was timely as the stocks of brandy declined in the 1870s and 1880s as a result of the phylloxera blight in France.

The 1890s was a period of unprecedented growth. New malt distilleries were opened and commercial groups like Distillers and the

North British Distillery Company, serving the interests of the grain distillers and the blenders respectively, became phenomenally successful.

Blending whisky is a highly developed skill: each brand is made to a specific recipe. Well-known brands like Famous Grouse and Bell's may have as many as 20–50 different whiskies in their make-up. Blending assembles the best degrees of whisky's richness – flavour, aroma, texture, mellowness and strength – without allowing any of the intrusive extremes of pungency, high strength, smokiness or blandness to dominate. Like sherry and champagne, the blend aspires to improvement rather than merely making something acceptable out of constituents that are unbalanced or flawed. Whiskies used in blended Scotch are available as whiskies in their own right and good blends will have 45–60 per cent malt content.

Alternative recipes have developed on the safe foundation of mainstream blended Scotch. De luxe blends are recognized as of superior quality, usually with a higher proportion of better-quality, longer-matured malts. They command substantial premiums, especially in export markets. There are also liqueurs based on blended whisky, for instance flavoured with honey, fruits, herbs and spices or cream (Drambuie, Glayva, Heather Cream).

TECHNIQUE:

Grain distilleries use continuous patent stills. The process is similar to that of making malt whisky up to the point of distillation, although everything takes place on a much larger scale and with much less malted barley. Distillation is carried out in 2 large cylindrical columns which are linked by pipes. The wash passes into the first column, the rectifier, in a coiled pipe running through its length. Jets of steam are forced up into the column through a series of perforated plates between which the coiled pipe passes, heating the wash inside before it passes out and into the analyser. In the analyser the wash is no longer in the coiled pipe, and it is now met by another jet of steam passing through more perforated plates.

The steam and evaporated alcohol rise and are passed back into the rectifier, cooling as it moves up, encountering fresh cold wash in the coiled pipe on the way down, until it reaches a cold water coil where it condenses before passing out to the still. The impure alcohols in the first and last part of the distillate can be redistilled while the alcohol which reaches the spirit safe and receiver is very pure. The whisky will mature faster than malt and is less subject to variable factors.

Blended whisky will be married in oak (often sherry) casks for at least a year to allow intermingling and further maturation to take place. As with most malts, the blend is reduced to the correct strength with the addition of water. There are at least 2,000 commercial blends. The major blenders own both grain and malt distilleries. All grain distilleries are located in the Lowlands of Scotland with the exception of Invergordon. Blending occurs throughout the country.

REGION OF PRODUCTION:
SCOTLAND.

Malt Whisky

DESCRIPTION:

MALT WHISKY HAS SPECIFIC, SOMETIMES VERY PRONOUNCED, FLAVOURS AND AROMAS WHICH COME FROM A NUMBER OF FACTORS: THE QUALITY OF THE WATER, THE MALTED BARLEY, THE AMOUNT OF PEAT USED IN DRYING THE GRAIN, THE SHAPE OF THE POT STILL, THE TYPE OF WOOD IN WHICH IT MATURES, THE LENGTH OF TIME IT HAS MATURED AND THE TEMPERATURE AND HUMIDITY CONDITIONS DURING MATURATION. THE RANGE OF CHARACTER GOES FROM DEEP, PUNGENT, SMOKY AND EARTHY TO LIGHT, SUBTLE, GENTLE AND SWEET. COLOUR IS PALE STRAW TO DEEP GOLD. MALT IS AROUND 40 PER CENT PROOF.

DISTINCTION IS MADE BETWEEN HIGHLAND AND LOWLAND MALTS. THE DIVIDING LINE IS THE HIGHLAND BOUNDARY FAULT WHICH RUNS FROM THE FIRTH OF CLYDE IN THE WEST TO THE FIRTH OF TAY. IN THE HIGHLAND AREA THERE ARE FURTHER DIFFERENCES: SPEYSIDERS HAVE

THEIR MELLOW, MALTY SWEETNESS; CAMPBELTOWN'S LIGHTLY PEATY MELLOWNESS COMPARES WITH ISLAY'S NOTABLY STRONGER PEATY FLAVOURS; NORTH HIGHLAND MALTS FROM INVERNESS TO WICK HAVE A DRY FRUITY-SWEETNESS, NOT NOTICEABLY PEATY; THE SOUTHERN MALTS NEAR PERTHSHIRE AND TO THE WEST ARE SOFT, LIGHT IN CHARACTER, OFTEN SWEET BUT SOME QUITE DRY; THE SMALL NUMBER OF WEST HIGHLAND MALTS BETWEEN OBAN AND FORT WILLIAM ARE SMOOTH AND ROUNDED; THE EASTERN HIGHLAND MALTS ALONG THE NORTH SEA COAST FROM BRECHIN TO BANFF HAVE A WIDE RANGE OF STYLES FROM FRUITY-SWEET TO PEATY-DRY; THE ISLAND MALTS OF JURA, MULL, SKYE AND ORKNEY (EXCLUDING ISLAY) HAVE A WIDE RANGE FROM DRY TO FULL, SWEET AND MALTY. LOWLAND MALTS ARE GENERALLY LESS ASSERTIVE; SOFT, LIGHT WITH A GENTLE SWEETNESS.

IN DESCRIBING A BOTTLE, THE TERM SINGLE MALT INDICATES WHISKY PRODUCED BY AN INDIVIDUAL DISTILLERY, WHILE VATTED MALT IS A BLEND FROM 2 OR MORE.

HISTORY:

The Scots word whisky derives from the Gaelic *uisge beatha* meaning water of life – in Latin *aqua vitae* – the common European root words for distilled spirit. While its origins in Scotland are hazy, its fortunes have had some dramatic ups and downs since the first written reference in 1494 in the Scottish Exchequer Rolls as a commercial product made in monasteries: 'eight bolls of malt to Friar John Cor wherewith to make aquavitae.'

The particular connection of malt whisky with the Highlands was a result of enthusiasm for home distilling, to use surplus barley and produce a warming drink against a cold, inhospitable climate. It was drunk with meals at least 3 times a day and commonly given as a restorative to children.

In every Highland glen sacks of barley would be soaked in water, possibly in the burn, for a few days to soften the grain and begin germination. Then the grain would be spread to allow it to sprout, halted by drying over a peat fire. The malted grain would then go into a large tub with boiling water and yeast to ferment. Once fermented, it would be passed twice through the pot still and the middle cut (the drinkable part, without the dangerous methyl alcohols) would be separated from the foreshots and the aftercuts or feints. It was a skilled operation which produced a liquor strongly influenced by the local water and peat and much more highly esteemed than anything distilled in the Lowlands. The Highlanders' distilling activities grew and developed until the Union in 1707 when the government began to tax them. For over 100 years, until the Excise Act in 1823, the Highlanders smuggled their malted whisky illicitly with great ingenuity. But the passing of the act signalled the beginning of a new era of development and success for the Highlanders' malt whisky as old smugglers became legitimate and linked their considerable skills to the business of large-scale production.

For the rest of the century and until about the 1920s the malt distilleries flourished. The First World War, prohibition in America and then the Second World War and its aftermath, meant a slump which lasted until the 1950s. Thereafter, an export-led recovery was under way. New distilleries were built in the 1960s, old ones reopened and the production of malt whisky quadrupled in a decade. This upturn in fortunes has, on the whole, continued, with an emphasis on quality and individual character as the range and variety of distinctive malts has become more widely appreciated.

TECHNIQUE:

The barley is soaked, spread out on the malting floor and turned daily until it sprouts. Germination is stopped by drying over a peat fire in a malt kiln. It is milled roughly and put into a mash tun and mixed with hot water until its sugars are dissolved producing a wort, when the solid remains of the barley are removed. The wort is cooled and mixed with yeast which converts it in about 2 days to a low-strength, alcoholic liquor known as the wash. This passes through first the wash still and then the spirit still, the middle cut is separated from the feints and foreshots and the spirit transferred to a vat to be mixed with water before transferring to casks where it must mature for 3 years before sale. Most will mature 8–15 years.

REGION OF PRODUCTION:
SCOTLAND.

Heather Honey

DESCRIPTION:

THIS IS SELDOM SOLD AS SINGLE-HEATHER HONEY, BUT LING HEATHER HONEY CAN BE DISTINGUISHED FROM THE OTHERS BY ITS THICK, JELLY-LIKE (THIXOTROPIC) CONSISTENCY WITH A STRONG AROMA AND FLAVOUR. HONEY FROM BELL HEATHER IS THINNER, WITH A MORE BITTER EDGE, WHILE CROSSLEAVED GIVES A THIN HONEY WITH LIGHTER FLAVOUR.

HISTORY:

Honey as a sweetener in the Scottish diet combines particularly well with the distinctive flavours of oatmeal and whisky in a number of drinks and dishes. Originally it was collected from wild colonies of bees: 'The boys,' says Osgood Mackenzie in *A Hundred Years in the Highlands* (1921), 'were able to collect large quantities of wild honey, which, by applying heat to it, was run into glass bottles and sold at the Stornoway markets. Hunting for wild-bee nests was one of the great ploys for the boys in the autumn … Cameron tells me that, as a young boy, before he left his home, there was an island in Loch Bhacha Chreamha where there was no necessity for hunting for bees' nests, as the whole island seemed under bees, the nests almost touching each other in the moss at the roots of tall heather … My stalker, too, informs me that his home at Kernsary used to be quite famous for its wild bees, but they finally disappeared.'

Beekeeping, which originated as a hobby or sideline for people running other businesses, continues to attract an enthusiastic following. The flavour of heather honey is highly esteemed for its distinctive character.

To ensure purity, hives are filled with unused combs and 'flitted' each summer, as the heather comes into bloom around the middle of July, to positions on the heather moors where the bees can collect the maximum nectar in the shortest time. To extract the honey, the outer caps are shaved off and the combs subjected to a Honey Loosener (nylon needles with a bulbous end which disturbs the honey). The combs are then put into a Tangential Swinging Basket Reversible which extracts by alternating 2 slow swinging movements with 2 fast. The honey is sieved into barrels and seeded (mixed with about a tenth volume of honey of the correct texture from the previous year's harvest) before it is poured into jars. Combs are cut and boxed.

PRODUCTION:

An average amount of honey per hive can vary from 350g to 69kg with the average working out at 23–30kg. A medium to large producer will have 300–400 hives.

REGION OF PRODUCTION:
SCOTLAND.

Oatmeal

DESCRIPTION:

COMPOSITION: WHOLE OATS, LESS THE HUSK. COLOUR: GREYISH-BEIGE. FLAVOUR: SWEET-MEALY, THIS DEPENDS ON THE MOISTURE AND OIL CONTENT, DETERMINED BY THE VARIETY, THE DISTRICT WHERE IT IS GROWN, THE SOIL AND THE CLIMATE.

HISTORY:

It is not known where or when cultivated oats originated. The first evidence of the grain in Scotland is carbonized grain found at archaeological excavations along the Forth and Clyde Canal dated to approximately 100 BC. It is generally agreed that although oats thrive best in cool climates, they originally came from some warmer country to the east. In a climate such as Scotland's, growth is comparatively slow which allows the kernels to fill out and mature better.

Oats became the most important food grain in Scotland towards the end of the seventeenth century when they displaced barley. Oatmeal was more versatile and was generally better liked for its flavour when made into oatcakes, porridge and brose, the staple items of the peasant diet. By the end of the eighteenth century oatmeal had become firmly established as the people's grain. 'Oatmeal with milk, which they cook in different ways, is their constant food, three times a day, throughout the year, Sundays and holidays included,' says Donaldson in *A General View of Agriculture of the Carse of Gowrie* (1794). Throughout the nineteenth century its popularity continued to increase. The figure of the penniless Scottish university scholar, surviving on his sack of oatmeal, is legendary. The mid-term holiday known as 'Meal Monday' was given to allow the student to return home to replenish his supply of oatmeal.

With the industrial revolution and the extension northwards of the English diet of cheap white bread accompanied by tea, the old oatmeal traditions of porridge, brose and oatcakes were seriously under threat. The fact that they have survived is largely to do with a greater understanding of the nutritional value of oatmeal as its role as a popular 'health' food has become established. Rolled oats, or oatflakes, were developed in America by the Quaker Oat company in 1877: they are made by steaming and rolling pinhead oatmeal. Their introduction greatly eased the process of making porridge and other oatmeal dishes.

There are several water-powered stone-ground mills as well as factory mills kiln-drying and stone-grinding oatmeal in the traditional way.

TECHNIQUE:

The traditional method is first to dry or condition the grain to a moisture content of usually around 15 per cent. It is then spread on a kiln floor, consisting of perforated metal sheets, with a smokeless-fuel furnace some 20–30 feet below. The oats are turned by hand with large shovels until the moisture content is reduced to around 4–5 per cent when the meal has taken on its mild nutty flavour. Milling begins with shelling the husks, then the grains are ground between stones to the required cuts or grades: pinhead (whole grain split into two) – used for haggis; rough – used for porridge, brose and sometimes oatcakes; medium/rough (sometimes known as coarse/medium) – used by butchers for mealie puddings; medium – used for porridge, brose, skirlie and baking; fine and super fine – used in baking and for feeding to babies.

REGION OF PRODUCTION:
SCOTLAND.

Scotland

South Scotland, North Scotland,
Scotland Countrywide

Address Book

Trade Associations and Interest Groups

Asparagus Growers Associaton www.british-asparagus.co.uk
Association of Master Bakers www.masterbakers.co.uk
Association of Scottish Shellfish Growers www.assg.co.uk
Bee Farmers Association www.beefarmers.co.uk
Biscuit, Cake, Chocolate and Confectionary Alliance
www.bcca.org.
Bramley Apple Information Service www.bramleyapples.co.uk
Bee Keepers Association www.bbka.org.uk
British Carrot Growers Association www.bcga.info
British Cheese Board www.cheeseboard.co.uk
British Deer Farmers Association www.bdfa.co.uk
British Goose Producers Association www.goose.cc
British Herb Trade Association www.bhta.org.uk
British Pig Association www.britishpigs.co.uk
British Summer Fruits www.britishsummerfruits.co.uk
British Soft Drinks Association www.britishsoftdrinks.com
British Waterfowl Association www.waterfowl.org.uk
Brogdale Horticultural Trust www.brogdale.org
Campaign for Real Ale www.camra.org.uk

Carrot Growers Association www.bcga.info

Common Ground www.england-in-particular.info

Curry Club www.thecurryclub.org.uk

Dairy Trade Federation www.dairyuk.org

English Apples and Pears www.englishapplesandpears.co.uk

English Farm Cider Centre www.middlefarm.com

Food from Britain www.foodfrombritain.co.uk

Food and Drink Federation www.fdf.org.uk

Game Conservancy Trust www.gct.org.uk

Gin and Vodka Association of Great Britain
www.ginvodka.org

Guild of Q Butchers www.guildofqbutchers.com

Henry Doubleday Research Association
(organic gardening and food) www.gardenorganic.org.uk

Herb Society www.herbsociety.co.uk

Kentish Cobnuts Association
www.kentishcobnutsassciation.co.uk

Meat and Livestock Commission www.mlc.org.uk

National Fruit Collection www.webvalley.co.uk

National Association of Cider Makers www.cideruk.com

National Farmers Union www.nfuonline.com

National Federation of Women's Institutes
www.womens-institute.co.uk

National Market Traders Federation www.nmtf.co.uk

National Sheep Association www.nationalsheep.org.uk

Quality Meat Scotland www.qmscotland.co.uk

Rare Breeds Survival Trust www.rbst.org.uk

Sausage Appreciation Society www.sausagefans.com

Scotch Malt Whisky Society www.smws.com

Scottish Association of Master Bakers www.samb.co.uk

Scottish Association of Meat Wholesalers
www.scottish-meat-wholesalers.org.uk

Scottish Crop Research Institute www.scri.sari.ac.uk

SCOTTISH FEDERATION OF MEAT TRADERS ASSOCIATION
www.sfmta.co.uk

SCOTTISH QUALITY SALMON www.scottishsalmon.co.uk

SEA FISH INDUSTRY AUTHORITY www.seafish.org.uk

SEASONING AND SPICE ASSOCIATION (UK)
www.seasoningandspice.org.uk

SHELLFISH ASSOCIATION OF GREAT BRITAIN www.shellfish.org.uk

SOIL ASSOCIATION www.soilassociation.org

SOUTH-WEST OF ENGLAND CIDER MAKERS ASSOCIATION
http://tinyurl.com/pylmg

SPECIALIST CHEESEMAKERS ASSOCIATION
www.specialistcheesemakers.co.uk

TASTE OF SHROPSHIRE www.shropshiretourism.info/food-and-drink/

TASTE OF THE WEST www.tasteofthewest.co.uk

TASTE OF WALES LTD www.wela.co.uk

TASTES OF ANGLIA LTD www.tastesofanglia.com

THREE COUNTIES CIDER AND PERRY ASSOCIATION
www.thethreecountiesciderandperryassociation.co.uk

TRADITIONAL FARM FRESH TURKEY ASSOCIATION
www.golden-promise.co.uk

UK TEA COUNCIL www.teacouncil.co.uk

UNITED KINGDOM VINEYARDS ASSOCIATION
www.englishwineproducers.com

WATERCRESS GROWERS ASSOCIATION www.watercress.co.uk

WINE AND SPIRIT TRADE ASSOCIATION www.wsta.co.uk

PRODUCERS, SUPPLIERS AND PARTICULAR INTEREST GROUPS

This is by no means an exhaustive list, but this list will point readers wishing to sample a taste of Britain in the right direction. Where possible, a website is given. For smaller organizations or individuals without a functioning website, a postal address is given.

The address book echoes the structure of the text, organized into categories that roughly reflect the natural order of a visit to market: fruit and vegetables, dairy, fishmonger, butchery, bakery, confectioners, drinks and condiments.

Fruit

SCOTTISH RASPBERRY
Scottish Crop Research Institute, (SCRI), Invergowrie, Dundee DD2 5DA.

Vegetables

KALE
Scottish Crop Research Institute, (SCRI), Invergowrie, Dundee DD2 5DA.
TOMATOES (SCOTLAND)
Scottish Crop Research Institute, (SCRI), Invergowrie, Dundee DD2 5DA.
British Tomato Growers Association, Pollards Nursery, Lake Lane, Barnham, W Sussex PO22 0AD.
VEGETARIAN HAGGIS
MacSween   www.macsween.co.uk

Dairy Produce

Milk, Cream, Butter And Ice Cream

Ayrshire milk
Ayrshire Cattle Society www.ayrshirescs.org

The Tally's ice-cream
Rizza's www.rizza.co.uk

Cheese

Caboc cheese
Highland Fine Cheeses, Knockbreck, Tain, Easter Ross 1V19 1LZ.

Crowdie cheese
Highland Fine Cheeses, Knockbreck, Tain, Easter Ross 1V19 1LZ.

Dunlop cheese
Ann Dorward, West Clerkland Farm Stewarton, Ayrshire KA3 5LP.
Scottish Handmakers Association, Walston Braehead Farm,
Carnwath, Lanarkshire
ML11 8NE.

Dunsyre Blue cheese
Handmade Cheeses of Scotland, Walston Braehead Farm, Carnwath,
Lanarkshire, ML11 8NE.

Kelsae cheese
Brenda Leddy, Garden Cottage Farm, Stitchill, Kelso TD5 7TL.

Fish & Seafood

Air-dried salted fish
MacCallum's of Troon, 71 Holdsworth St, Finnieston, Glasgow.

Arbroath smokie
R.R. Spink www.rrspink.com

Finnan haddock
Andy Race, Fish Merchants Ltd www.andyrace.co.uk

Kipper (Scottish cure)

Summer Isles Foods www.summerislesfoods.com

LOCH FYNE SMOKEHOUSE www.lochfyne.com

MUSSEL (SCOTLAND)

The Scottish Shellfish Marketing Group www.scottishshellfish.co.uk

OYSTER (SCOTLAND)

Loch Fyne Oysters www.lochfyne.com

SMOKED EEL

The Teviot Game Fare Smokery www.teviotgamefaresmokery.co.uk

Summer Isles Foods www.summerislesfoods.com

SMOKED SALMON (SCOTLAND)

Scotfood Ltd, Clachan, Locheport, Lochmaddy,
North Uist PA82 5ET.

Summer Isles Foods www.summerislesfoods.com

Hebridean Smokehouse Ltd www.hebrideansmokehouse.com

SPOOT

Orkney Fishermen's Society www.ofsorkney.co.uk

Meat

CATTLE

ABERDEEN-ANGUS CATTLE

Aberdeen-Angus Cattle Society www.aberdeen-angus.co.uk

BEEF SHORTHORN CATTLE

Beef Shorthorn Society
www.shorthorn.co.uk/beef_shorthorn/home.htm

GALLOWAY CATTLE

The Galloway Cattle Society www.gallowaycattlesociety.co.uk

HIGHLAND CATTLE

The Highland Cattle Society www.highlandcattlesociety.com

MacBeth, Butchers www.macbeths.com

SHEEP

CHEVIOT SHEEP

P. Francis, Secretary, Brecknock Hill Cheviot Sheep Society,
13 Lion Street, Brecon, Powys LD3 7HY.
Cheviot Sheep Society www.cheviotscheep.org
North Country Cheviot Sheep Society
www.nc-cheviot.co.uk/public.index.php

NORTH RONALDSAY SHEEP

The National Farmers Union www.nfuonline.com/x11.xml

SHETLAND SHEEP

The Shetland Sheep Society www.users.zetnet.co.uk/ssbg/index.html

SNAILS AND GAME

RED DEER VENISON AND RED GROUSE

Weatherall Foods Ltd. www.blackface.co.uk
Highland Game www.highlandgame.com

Meat Products

AYRSHIRE BACON

Ramsay of Carluke www.ramsayofcarluke.co.uk

FORFAR BRIDIES

JAS McLaren & Sons, 22 Market Street, Forfar, Scotland.

HAGGIS

MacSween www.acsween.co.uk

POTTED MEAT

Heal Farm www.healfarm.co.uk

SCOTCH PIES

Scotsmeat www.scotsmeat.com
H. R. Bradsfords Bakers, 70 Spiersbridge Road, Thornliebank,
Glasgow G46 7SN.

Smoked game

Rannoch Smokery www.rannocksmokery.co.uk

Summer Isles Foods, Achiltibuie, Ullapool, Wester Ross IV26 2YG.

Breads

Beremeal bannocks

Orkney Quality Food and Drink Ltd www.oqfd.co.uk

Puggie buns

Fisher and Donaldson www.fisheranddonaldson.com

Selkirk bannocks

A. Dalgetty & Sons www.alex-dalgetty.co.uk

Softie

Chalmers Bakery, Auchmill Road, Bucksburn, Aberdeen AB21 9LB.

Square loaf

Chalmers Bakery, Auchmill Road, Bucksburn, Aberdeen AB21 9LB.

Griddle-breads, biscuits & Puddings

Abernethy biscuit

Simmers www.nairns-oatcakes.com/simmers/simmers_index.html

Clootie dumpling

A. Dalgetty & Sons Bakers www.alex-dalgetty.co.uk

Speyside Heather Centre Clootie Dumpling

http://heathercentre.com/acatalog/Clootie_Dumplings.html

Kirriemuir gingerbread

Bells Bakers www.bellbakers.co.uk

Paving stone

Fisher and Donaldson www.fisheranddonaldson.com

Petticoat tails

The Shortbread House of Edinburgh www.shortbreadhouse.com

Raggy biscuit

Fisher and Donaldson www.fisheranddonaldson.com

Scottish oatcake

Stockan & Gardens www.stockan-and-gardens.co.uk

Shortbread

The Shortbread House of Edinburgh www.shortbreadhouse.com

Cakes & Pies

Cumnock tart

H.R. Bradford (Bakers) 70 Spiersbridge Road, Thornliebank, Glasgow G46 7SN.

Dundee cake

Goodfellow & Steven www.scottishbaking.co.uk

Confectionery

Edinburgh rock

Gibbs, Fort Matilda, Greenock PA16 7SZ.

Ross's of Edinburgh, Pentland Industrial Estate, Loanhead, Edinburgh EH20 9QR.

Hawick balls

Gibbs, Fort Matilda, Greenock PA16 7SZ.

Humbugs

Humbugs Traditional Sweet Shop www.humbuguk.co.uk

Jeddart snails

Millers, 10 High Street, Jedburgh, Roxburghshire TD8 6AG.

Moffat toffee

The Moffat Toffee Shop

www.dalbeattie.com/moffat/traders/moffat-toffee/index.html

Starry rock

The Star Rock Shop www.thestarrockshop.co.uk

Tablet

The Moffat Toffee Shop, High Street, Moffat, Scotland DG10 9DW.

Aromatics & Condiments

Marmalade

Pettigrews of Kelso www.pettigrews.com

Rowan jelly

Moniack Castle and Highland Wineries www.moniackcastle.co.uk

Flours

Beremeal

Golspie Mill Sutherland www.golspiemill.co.uk

Barony Mill, Birsay, Orkney KW17 2LY.

Oatmeal

The Oatmeal of Alford www.oatmealofalford.com

Beverages

Ginger wine

Stone's of London www.stonesgingerwine.com

Matthew Clark www.matthewclark.co.uk

Heather ale

Heather Ale, New Alloa Brewery, Kelliebank, Alloa FK10 1NU.

Irn-Bru

A.G. Barr plc www.agbarr.co.uk

MALT WHISKY
Bowmore Distillery www.morrisonbowmore.com
SCOTTISH CASK-CONDITIONED BEER OR ALE
Traquair House Brewery www.traquair.co.uk
Broughton Brewery Ltd www.broughtonales.co.uk
SILVER BIRCH WINE
Highland Wineries www.moniackcastle.co.uk
Broadland Wineries Ltd www.broadland-wineries.co.uk

PGOS AND PGIS

Britain and continental Europe possess an enormous range of wonderful food. When a product's reputation extends beyond national borders, however, it can find itself in competition with products using the same name and passing themselves off as genuine. This unfair competition discourages producers and misleads consumers, and for this reason the European Union in 1992 created systems known as Protected Designation of Origin and Protected Geographical Indication to promote and protect regionally important food products. A Protected Designation of Origin (PDO) describes a food that is produced, processed and prepared in a given geographical area, using a recognised skill. A Protected Geographical Indication (PGI) demonstrates a geographical link between a foodstuff and a specific region in at least one of the stages of production, processing or preparation.

For more information, visit

http://ec.europa.eu/agriculture/qual/en/uk_en.htm

Bibliography

Unless otherwise indicated, the place of publication is London and the country of publication is the United Kingdom.

Allen, Brigid (1994) ed., *Food*, Oxford University Press.

Banfeld, W.T. (1947), 'Manna', *A Comprehensive Treatise on Bread Manufacture* (2nd ed.), Maclaren.

Beeton, Isabella (1861), *Beeton's Book of Household Management*, facsimile ed. 1982, Chancellor Press.

Bond, R. (1923), *The Ship's Baker*, Munro, Glasgow.

Cassell's (1896), *Cassell's Dictionary of Cookery* (first ed. c. 1875).

Bradley, Martha (1756), *The British Housewife*, facsimile ed. 1997-8, Prospect Books, Totnes.

Buchanan, G. (1629), *Description of Scotland*.

Cassell's (1896), *Cassell's Dictionary of Cookery* (first ed. c. 1875).

Cherfas, J. (1995), 'Vanishing Potatoes, not an illusion', *Disappearing Foods*, Oxford Symposium on Food and Cookery, ed. Harlan Walker, Prospect Books, Totnes.

Clark, Lady (1909), *The Cookery Book of Lady Clark of Tillypronie*, ed. 1994, Southover Press, Lewes.

Clark, Colette, ed. (1960), *Home at Grasmere*, Penguin Books.

Cleland, E. (1755), *A New and Easy Method of Cookery*, Edinburgh.

David, Elizabeth (1968),(1977), *English Bread and Yeast Cookery*, Allen Lane.

'Dods, Meg' ['Dods, Mrs Margaret, of the Cleikum Inn, St Ronan's'] (1826), *The Cook and House-wife's Manual*, Edinburgh. (Written anonymously by Christian Isobel Johnstone.)

Dyson, John (1977), *Business in Great Waters*, Angus and Robertson.

Fenton, A. (1973), 'Traditional Elements in the diet of the Northern Isles of Scotland', Reports from the Second International Symposium for Ethnological Food Research, Helsinki.

Glasse, Hannah (1747), *The Art of Cookery Made Plain and Easy*, facsimile 1983, Prospect Books.

Hartley, Dorothy (1954), *Food in England*, Macdonald and Janes.

Grigson, Jane (1971), *Good Things*, Michael Joseph.

——— (1974), *English Food*, Macmillan.

——— (1975), *Fish Cookery*, Penguin Books.

——— (1982), *Fruit*, Michael Joseph.

——— (1984), *Observer Guide to British Cookery*, Michael Joseph.

Hall, S.J.G. and Clutton-Brock, J. (1989), *Two Hundred Years of British Farm Livestock*, British Museum.

Hope, Annette (1987), *A Caledonian Feast*, Mainstream Publishing, Edinburgh.

Jamieson, Dr J. (1818), *Dictionary of the Scottish Language*.

Kirkland, J. (1907), *The Modern Baker, Confectioner and Caterer*, Gresham Publishing Company.

Mabey, David (1978), *In Search of Food, traditional eating and drinking in Britain*, Macdonald and Jane's.

MacCarthy, D. (1989), *Food Focus 1*, Food From Britain.

MacClure, Victor (1955), *Good Appetite, My Companion*, Odhams.

Mackay, C. (1888), *Dictionary of Lowland Scots*.

McKee, R. (1991), 'Ice Cream Vendors', *Public Eating*, Oxford Symposium on Food and Cookery, ed. Harlan Walker, Prospect Books, Totnes.

Mackenzie, Compton (1954), *Echoes*, Chatto & Windus.

MacLean, Donald (n.d.), *Potato Varieties, a Fact sheet on Special Properties*.

May, Robert (1660), *The Accomplisht Cook*, facsimile ed., 1994, Prospect Books, Totnes.

McLintock, Mrs (1736), *Mrs McLintock's Receipts for Cookery and Pastry Work*, facsimile ed., Aberdeen University Press with an introduction by Iseabail Macleod.

McNeill, F.M. (1929), *The Scots Kitchen*, Blackie, Glasgow.

Markham, Gervase (1615), *The English Hus-wife*.

May, Robert (1660), *The Accomplisht Cook*, facsimile ed., 1994, Prospect Books, Totnes.

Raffald, E. (1769), *The Experienced English Housekeeper*, facsimile of 1782 ed. 1970, E&W Books.

Rance, Patrick (1982), *The Great British Cheese Book*, Macmillan.

Simon, A.L. (1960), *The Concise Encyclopaedia of Gastronomy*, Collins (1983 ed., Penguin Books).

Stead, Jennifer (1991), 'Prodigal Frugality', *Traditional Food East and West of the Pennines*, ed. C.A. Wilson, Edinburgh University Press.

Stobart, Tom (1977), *Herbs, Spices and Flavourings*, Penguin.

——— (1980), *The Cook's Encyclopaedia*, Batsford.

Stocker, D. (1988), P*otted Tales, Recollections and views of Morecambe Bay Fishermen*, Lancaster City Museums, Lancaster.

Thompson, E.P. (1975), *Whigs and Hunters*, Penguin Books.

Wordsworth, Dorothy (1803), R*ecollections of a Tour Made in Scotland*.

Acknowledgements

Scotland Countrywide, North Scotland, South Scotland
From Petticoat Tails to Arbroath Smokies
Traditional Foods of Scotland

Particular thanks to the following chefs, authors and journalists who generously contributed pieces to the book:

Gordon Ramsay (p.69-71), Catherine Brown (p.83-5), Tom Lewis (p.111), Sue Lawrence (p.132-3).

The following people have kindly given the compilers information about particular foods and trades. This book could not have been completed without their assistance.

B. Bertram, Kirriemuir, Scotland; N. Fletcher, Auchtermuchty, Fife; J. Hamilton, Annan, Scotland; W. Morrison, Tain, Rossshire; G. Ross, Edinburgh; B. Williams, Glasgow.